CROSSING *the* DIVIDE

from Baptist *to* Latter-day Saint

What others are saying about

CROSSING *the* DIVIDE

CROSSING THE DIVIDE is a delightful and engaging autobiography that chronicles what every true conversion should be—Spirit-directed and profoundly life-changing. Bryan Ready has written a page-turner that I found hard to set down. As he tells his own conversion story, first to Christ and later to His restored gospel, Bryan teaches us how we can be better Christians, better missionaries, and more focused on Christ in our faith, our testimonies, and the way we live our lives. I recommend Crossing the Divide. It will almost assuredly help you to bridge the gap between where you are spiritually, and where you can be.

—Alonzo L. Gaskill, professor
World Religions, Brigham Young University

ONE OF THE PRECIOUS TRUTHS that is affirmed so powerfully in this remarkable conversion story is how our loving Lord works on and with each one of us, leading us along, one step at a time, bit by bit, dispensing a sacred truth here and planting a quiet but persuasive witness there. The conversion of our dear friend, Bryan Ready, is a story that every Latter-day Saint and, for that matter, every follower of Christ, ought to read. It is a testament to how the Good Shepherd, in His own time and in His own way, will lead His sheep to the fullness of His gospel.

—Robert L. Millet, professor emeritus
Ancient Scripture, Brigham Young University

CROSSING *the* DIVIDE

from Baptist *to* Latter-day Saint

BRYAN READY

CFI
An imprint of Cedar Fort, Inc.
Springville, Utah

ISBN 13: 978-1-4621-4074-9

Published by CFI, an imprint of Cedar Fort, Inc.
2373 W. 700 S., Springville, UT 84663
Distributed by Cedar Fort, Inc., www.cedarfort.com

Library of Congress Control Number: 2021939675

Cover design by Courtney Proby

Edited and typeset by Valene Wood

Printed in the United States of America

10 9 8 7 6 5 4 3 2 1

Printed on acid-free paper

Dedicated to my parents,
Raymond (Gene) Ready and Pamela Ready,
whose family visits to Temple Square, Nauvoo,
and Osmond concerts began this journey.

Contents

Foreword

Dr. Shon D. Hopkin

As I was working on this foreword in May 2021, I received news from Bryan's oldest son, BJ, that he and his father had been in a life-altering automobile accident. While driving on an open stretch of country road in his home state of Illinois, a vehicle inexplicably ran a stop sign and hit Bryan's side of the car, with BJ in the passenger seat. BJ had serious injuries, including broken ribs and damage to internal organs. These were treated and BJ left the hospital to recover later that week. Bryan's injuries, on the other hand, left him in critical condition for a number of days. Surgeries on his upper back, pelvis, and other areas of his body saved his life, but Bryan's recovery is moving slowly at the time I am writing this. Rehab processes are difficult, since a broken pelvis and arm mean that moving with a walker is more akin to gingerly hopping with a walker.

As of yesterday, 10 May 2021, Bryan's voice is (temporarily, he hopes) raspy and soft, both from the accident and from the intubation that remained in his throat for a couple of weeks after the accident, reminding me immediately of President Spencer W. Kimball's voice after his throat surgery. His likeable, soft, southern twang, too mild to fit comfortably with caricature of the Southern Baptist preacher, has a bit of an otherworldly feel to it for now. He spoke with me about

God's will and learning the lessons God wishes to give us, even when it is difficult for us to understand them in the present moment. The timing of his accident—a couple of months after this book had been accepted by a publisher and only a week or so after an "All In" podcast interview with him had posted online—certainly led him to feel that the adversity may have been linked to this message being heard. He shared a story of a frightening night in the hospital when he believed he might not survive, feeling an otherworldly oppression and antagonism. The accident has sharpened his desire for his voice and story to receive an audience, and I am grateful that this book will be published without an immediate, mortal "The End" occasioned by his accident. Bryan still has much to add in the future, and his mortal road will continue to take the twists and turns that come to each of us, with steep climbs resulting in stunning vistas, possibly followed by long and sometimes lonely stretches of pavement, and hopefully culminating in a warm, joyful arrival at his heavenly destination when the time comes. I believe that God has a role for each of us to play, if we are willing, and that Bryan's role is unfolding in beautiful, complex, and powerful ways. I feel blessed to have been a small part of that inspiring journey thus far.

Although Bryan gives the story of our interaction in chapter 6, I will share my own perspective of how our friendship began and developed. About a year after being hired into the Ancient Scripture department at Brigham Young University, I was asked by Robert Millet if I would be willing to engage in an email interfaith discussion with Bryan Ready. Dr. Millet and I had worked on a number of interfaith projects together, including my service on the newly formed Religious Outreach Council that he chaired. We had traveled to Texas together to meet with a variety of pastors and academics focused on biblical studies, including a relatively large gathering in Austin, TX, where I met with dear friends from my PhD days at the University of Texas, Austin, which included service as a member and later as president of the University Interfaith Council at UT. When Dr. Millet came to ask me to dialogue with Bryan, I was very busy but still accepted enthusiastically.

Over the next few years, Bryan and I wrote back and forth frequently. Sometimes email responses would take a number of months, as each side thought about what to say and how to respond (and as the busy nature of life took over). From the beginning, Bryan was friendly in tone without pulling any punches about what he viewed as some of the challenges with Latter-day Saint theological views when compared with his understanding of biblical teachings. We discussed theological concepts of scriptural inerrancy, of relying solely upon the Bible (*sola scriptura*), of salvation by grace through faith in Christ alone, of agency and free will and the sovereignty of God, of the Book of Mormon, of Joseph Smith, of salvation (soteriology), and of dozens more topics.

Sometimes Bryan pushed hard in our dialogue in very well-intentioned ways, creating more of the debate atmosphere that some Latter-day Saints may find familiar from a few of their own conversations with deeply committed Evangelical Christians. At some of those times, I would push back fairly hard, but would then wonder if I had allowed my own feelings of deep commitment to get in the way of healthy dialogue and understanding. Communicating with Bryan was always a two-way street for both of us. I did not participate in the dialogue to teach Bryan how he should believe. Rather, I hoped to communicate how one (hopefully) thoughtful Latter-day Saint might understand the theological topics at hand. I wanted him to feel some of the beauty and attraction of Latter-day Saint beliefs from my own perspective, and to help him recognize that I had spent time thinking through some of the complexities and concerns that he articulated with regards to those beliefs. At the same time, I hoped to gain the same thing from my discussion with Bryan, a greater understanding of how he, as a theologically trained Southern Baptist pastor, might view concepts of potential dissonance between our two religious faiths. I wanted to understand why the concepts of scriptural inerrancy, or of the Trinity, or of *sola scriptura* were important and persuasive to him.

The task of understanding each other was made easier by Bryan's own familiarity with Latter-day Saint modes of thinking. He had a good sense for how and why I viewed the world as I did and had practice sharing his own theological understandings with members of the Church of Jesus Christ of Latter-day Saints. That being stated, this same familiarity at times made the discussion more challenging in positive ways. Bryan was trained to successfully debate scriptural topics, and his training was at its best when used with or against Latter-day Saints. Additionally, Bryan cared about the discussion in ways that were completely hidden from me. If he could not see a way to understand a Latter-day Saint position, he pushed on that problem again and again.

At the time of the discussion, this often was challenging and even tiring for me. I clearly remember numerous instances of staying up into the early hours of the morning, typing emailed responses to thoughts and questions that Bryan had raised, and wondering if this was really the best way for me to be using my time as a young, busy professor. I did not know that Bryan was seeking theological understanding to help him process the change he had been considering: baptism into the Church of Jesus Christ of Latter-day Saints. From that perspective, his articulate questions, challenges, and pushback look very different to me now. Bryan was never rude or unkind, much the opposite. But he was rarely if ever content with answers that avoided the actual crux of the matter.

Bryan's thoughts and insights into a variety of theological positions were instructive and helpful for me in ways that continue to benefit me today. When we are challenged to approach our own beliefs from angles that we have not previously considered, we find new elements and perspectives that are enriching and enhancing. This process of interfaith dialogue has rarely if ever challenged my belief in the teachings of the restored gospel. Rather, it has caused my belief and understanding to grow deeper and more nuanced in ways that I find incredibly satisfying. Bumping my own beliefs as a member of the Church into Bryan's beliefs that were developed over decades of Bible study and theological training has helped understand and appreciate my Baptist friends better, but even more it has helped me understand myself better. Working with Bryan prepared me to communicate more clearly in a number of areas. I have used thoughts that he shared with me at least two different times when writing books or articles. The first time I failed to properly cite Bryan's helpful insights, which I am happy to confess here in an attempt to ease my self-recrimination. At Brigham Young University I have often taught a Book of Mormon class designed for BYU students who are not members of the Church.

The experience has been thrilling and the teaching environment constantly keeps me on my toes. Many of my students have been Baptist, or Evangelical, or non-denominational Christians (along with numerous other branches of Christianity), and my dialogue with Bryan has been useful again and again in that space to understand my students' viewpoints and to communicate with them in ways that are as clear as possible.

Following months and then years of dialogue, Bryan caught me by surprise late one night when he sent me an email letting me know that he was considering being baptized. Never before that moment had I supposed such a thing. I learned that Bryan had been meeting with the missionaries for many years and had begun to believe, even before we began our discussions, that God may have been calling him to be baptized into the Church of Jesus Christ of Latter-day Saints. Some of his goals with our dialogue were to determine whether his mind could learn to give intellectual assent to the things that his heart was prompting to him to accept.

Bryan is completely loyal to the teachings of the restored gospel, but his many years of honest, committed theological training at times lead him to think about those teachings somewhat differently than other Latter-day Saints. He is comfortable with the teaching that the Godhead is three separate beings, but he is more inclined than most Latter-day Saints to remind those listening that the Godhead is also One in ways that we cannot fully comprehend. He is grateful for the emphasis on agency and free will in the Church, but his loyalty to and faith in the sovereignty of God lead him to understand that agency as an outgrowth of God's omnipotence and omniscience. Most Latter-day Saints would not find anything to disagree with in the previous sentence, but they might not have thought about the issue in quite the same way. Bryan's belief that his covenants and ordinances spring from a faith enabled by God's grace colors everything that he does as a member of the Church. Most importantly, he joins his own witness of Jesus Christ's redeeming love with those of his fellow members, reminding all who will listen that faith must be centered on Jesus Christ, not on any other human or concept, if it is to lead to salvation.

Later in this book, Bryan will tell the inspiring story of how he came to make the difficult decision to be baptized, even with competing previous commitments to "Jesus, Jennifer, and job." Prior to that time, I finally met him in person when he and his son, BJ, came to Utah to attend a General Conference and we were able to obtain seats that were fairly close to the front of the conference center. I still find it humorous that my Baptist pastor friend helped me sit as close to the front of General Conference as has ever been possible for me.

I remember clearly when he asked me to write a letter to his beloved Baptist congregation, explaining that Latter-day Saints believe in Jesus Christ as their Savior and that Bryan was, is, and will always be fully committed to that central belief no matter where his future path might take him. Bryan almost chose not to read that letter because of how shocking it would be to his congregation, but his son BJ's encouragement during an altar call at the end of a service—in which BJ told Bryan that he tried to resist coming up to tell his dad to read the email, but that he thought he was going to throw up if he did not do so—helped him take that incredibly challenging step that would eventually allow him to move forward with his desire to become a member of the Church.

Even after that moment, Bryan's path to baptism took many months and included pitfalls and stumbling stones. Many months later when I let Bryan know that I would be coming to St. Louis, Missouri for an academic conference, he asked me if I had any white clothing I could bring. That comment again caught me by surprise, and I was not sure if he was saying what I thought he was saying. Only upon arrival did he tell me of the miracles that God had worked over the preceding hours with his wife and family. What a joyous memory it was and will always be to have accompanied Bryan into the waters of baptism. When I later apologized that I had to perform the baptism twice to make sure that Bryan was completely immersed, he graciously told me that it gave him more time to appreciate the experience.

Since that day, Bryan has dealt with continued challenges from those that love him in his community and who struggle to understand his decision. He continues to weather these challenges with appreciation, grace, and good humor, even when bumping into someone who is surprised to see him because she heard that he had moved to Utah to marry multiple wives!

After our many years of dialogue, I am pleased to say that the theological discussion has continued, albeit at a slower pace. Bryan and I continue to discuss and debate doctrinal understandings in ways that still expand and challenge my thinking. I have anxiously waited for reports and summaries of Bryan's experiences as he received the Melchizedek priesthood, as he performed baptisms for the dead, as he received his patriarchal blessing, as he was endowed in the temple, and as he served in callings. Bryan loves his ward, even though he sometimes sees things a bit differently than some members of his Church community. The strongest critique I ever heard Bryan give was, "Shon, can you tell me why, if a hymn has a certain meter range indicated, we are determined to sing it at least ten beats a minute slower than the lowest speed given???!!!" I am guessing that some reading this may have dealt with similar feelings at times.

Bryan has come to lecture at BYU three times, both before and since his baptism, each time meeting with the friends on the Religion Faculty that he has formed over the years—Barbara Morgan Gardner, Mark Ellison, JB Haws, Andrew Skinner, Alonzo Gaskill, Robert Millet, and others. He has lectured to the BYU Religious Education faculty, to a room packed full of BYU students, and to a group of Faith Again attendees organized by Jay Griffiths in Salt Lake City. He has developed an ability to help Latter-day Saints whose faith in Christ is struggling. Each time he has visited Utah, he has brought different members of his family with him, and it has been a joy to get to know BJ, Carrie, and Caleb better during those visits, each of them remarkable and good in their own ways, as are Bryan and Jennifer's younger children. I have enjoyed frequent email conversations with BJ over the years, and my family has been the grateful recipient of boxes of Fitz's root beer, a product of St. Louis, sent by BJ as gifts for the past few years. BJ's own baptism story is also remarkable, and both Carrie and Caleb have developed strong friendships with members of the Church. They continue to bless many in the Church and to be blessed by them.

Each of our faith stories is unique, but I have been blessed to participate in Bryan's story in very personal ways. I believe that association and friendship will bless my life throughout the eternities. This would be true whether Bryan had been baptized as part of the story or not. The friendship has made me a better man and has encouraged me to be a better Latter-day Saint. I am confident that it will do the same for you as you enjoy Bryan's special whit, candor, and insight over the ensuing pages. May you be blessed by the story as I have been.

Dr. Shon D. Hopkin

Associate Professor of Religious Education
Chair, Department of Ancient Scripture

Fellow, Brigham Young University Council of Religious Outreach, 2014–2020
May 2021

Introduction

"I don't blame any one for not believing my history. If I had not experienced what I have, I would not have believed it myself."

—Joseph Smith Jr.

THOUSANDS OF PEOPLE ARE BAPTIZED INTO THE CHURCH OF JESUS Christ of Latter-day Saints every week. In many ways my story is no different than any other convert. Through the providence of God, we heard the gospel, gained a testimony of its truthfulness, and joined the Church. Each of us is a miracle of God's grace. Each story is also unique. My story is unique in two ways: First, I spent most of my life studying the teachings and history of the Church. I was a critic of the Church. I believed it was a cult and that Joseph Smith was a false prophet. Second, I was an ordained Southern Baptist pastor with a formal theological education. I was well aware of the theological divide that separated the restored gospel and traditional Christianity. I didn't think that divide could be bridged. Many others, both Latter-day Saint and traditional Christians, also believe that divide cannot be bridged. I now believe it can. This book tells the story of how I made that change.

This book came about as the result of a dialogue I've had with several members of Brigham Young University's Religious Education faculty for several years. In 2018, I was invited to BYU to speak to some students and faculty from the Religious Education Department. After hearing my presentation, several of them encouraged me to write a book about my experiences. This is the result. It's not that easy to write about yourself. And in many ways, this isn't my story. It's the story of God's work in my life. To Him be all the glory.

I hope that readers will come away with a greater reassurance that God can work and has been working this same way in the lives of countless other people. If the reader hasn't yet experienced God's amazing grace for themselves, I want them to know that they can. I hope this book inspires the reader to seek Him out.

I'm also writing this book with the hope that it might contribute to the ongoing dialogue between Latter-day Saint and other Christians. I've included an appendix to discuss some of the issues that divide us—specifically, some of the major issues I had to work through to transition from being a Southern Baptist pastor to a Latter-day Saint. I hope to show that we have a lot more in common then we might think. I hope this book will help readers understand some of these differences and show how we might be able to find common ground. As Western culture becomes more and more anti-Christian, it becomes more important for those of us with shared values to work together.

I also hope that this book might be beneficial to anyone currently investigating The Church of Jesus Christ of Latter-day Saints. If they are concerned about certain beliefs or the stories about Joseph Smith, this book will show them how I navigated these issues and may help them on their own journey.

Most importantly, I hope this book will point people to our Lord and Savior Jesus Christ and encourage them to enter into a relationship with Him.

A word on methodology. For the purposes of this book, the word "Church" will refer to The Church of Jesus Christ of Latter-day Saints unless it is obviously being used in reference to other faiths, e.g., Presbyterian Church, Baptist Church, etc. Scriptures from the Old and New Testaments are cited from the King James Version.

This book would not have been possible without the profound help of two amazing men, both of BYU's Religious Education faculty—Dr. Robert Millet for his encouragement and willingness to help me navigate the book-writing process; and Dr. Shon Hopkin, for his friendship, his patience as my dialogue partner, and his willingness to baptize me.

I would like to thank the team at Cedar Fort Publishing and Media for their willingness to take a chance on an unknown author and publish my story. Their hard work, suggestions, and guidance have made this book far better than I could have envisioned. I'd also like to thank them for their prayers and support as I recovered from my accident. I am incredibly grateful for these wonderful brothers and sisters.

I'd also like to thank my oldest son, Bryan Jacob Ready, my consigliere in all things related to the Church. He started his own study of the restored gospel when he was about fifteen years old. He went through the missionary discussions with me and joined the Church three years after I did.

I'd like to thank Dr. Alonzo Gaskill for including my story in a book he edited about those who converted to the Church from other faiths. The writing I did for his book laid the foundation for this one.

I'd like to thank my friends who took the time to read my manuscript and offer helpful suggestions: Lynn Ennis, Don Dubree, David Sylvester, and Deveri Thornton.

I'd like to thank the rest of my family: my children, Carrie, Caleb, Matthew, Kaylee, Rebekah; my wife, Jennifer; and my mother, Pam, for their willingness to let me drag them to countless Latter-day Saint historical sites and their patience while I studied and wrote. I love you.

And finally, I want to again thank my Lord and Savior Jesus Christ. Without Him there would be nothing.

Chapter 1

Beginnings

Jesus is the Son of God. He was born of the Virgin Mary in Bethlehem. He died on the Cross outside of Jerusalem. He arose from the grave. I cannot remember a time when I did not know those truths. My mother made sure I knew about Jesus. She taught me how to pray, and that God would answer my prayers. We did not attend church regularly. We went sporadically through the year but always on Christmas and Easter. In the summer months, I attended more Vacation Bible Schools than I could count.

I was born in October 1968 in Alton, Illinois (Alton is part of the greater St. Louis, Missouri metropolitan area). I grew up in Alton and neighboring Godfrey, Illinois. I had a very idyllic childhood. I grew up in a neighborhood surrounded by woods. My friends and I would roam all over the place when we weren't in school. We just had to stay in range of our mother's voice and come running when she called. It was a great time to grow up.

Music was always part of my life. I remember singing in public when I was six years old. I loved to sing, and I loved good harmony. The Osmond family excelled at both. They were extremely popular with my friends and me in the mid-1970s. The first 33-rpm record I bought was an Osmond record. I remember it had this weird looking record label, "Kolob Records." It appeared to have a reference to some scripture included with it, though I could never find it in the Bible. Over the next few years, I would continue to buy Osmond records.

In 1976, the Donny and Marie Show premiered and I would watch it every Friday night. I even joined their fan club. One year, their annual fan club mailing included a pamphlet entitled "This We Believe." It was the first time I remember seeing the names "Mormon," "Book of Mormon," and "The Church of Jesus Christ of Latter-day Saints." My mother let me read the pamphlet, and then she put it away. Apparently, there was something really weird about those folks.

Like many non-Latter-day Saints, my mother had heard about the "strange" things Latter-day Saints believed, and that they weren't "true" Christians. Some of her friends cautioned her about letting me listen to the Osmonds. But she appreciated their talent and their wholesome ways which contrasted with so much of the rest of pop music. So, she continued to buy me Osmond records and take me to their concerts when they performed nearby at the Mississippi River Festival or Illinois State Fair.

One year my parents decided to take a huge family vacation out west. We were going to visit the Rocky Mountains and Yellowstone, and on the way, we would stop in Utah and tour the Osmond Family Studios. It was so cool. We actually caught a brief glimpse of Donny & Marie in the studio. I still remember how tired they looked.

We spent the night in Salt Lake City. The next morning, we drove out to see the Great Salt Lake and then came back to tour Temple Square. I still remember walking up the ramp in the North Visitors Center to see the Christus statue. I remember seeing the temple lit up at night. And I remember my mother buying a Book of Mormon for a dollar at the visitors' center. It had a light blue cover with an angel blowing a trumpet on the front.

When we came home, my mother put that Book of Mormon on her bookshelf. I was continually drawn to this book. I don't know if it was the blue cover in contrast to the dark covers of the other books on the shelf, but every time I looked at the bookshelf, that book stood out to me. I would take it off the shelf and thumb its pages. I tried to read it but couldn't understand it. So, I just looked at the pictures and put it back on the shelf. Weeks, sometimes months, would pass and it would catch my eye again. This happened repeatedly until I received my own copy of the Book of Mormon later in high school.

A year after the family vacation, the Osmonds presented a fireside in nearby St. Louis, Missouri. In the fall of 1979, a Latter-day Saint friend invited my mother and me to attend the fireside featuring the Osmond family and baseball player Harmon Killebrew. I remember sitting about halfway back in the cultural hall listening to the Osmonds bear their testimonies. They talked about their faith in Jesus Christ, their belief in the restored gospel and the miracles that they had experienced. I was as impressed as a ten-year-old could be. I remember on the car ride home I was sitting in the back seat. I turned to my mother and said, "Mom, I want to be a Mormon." She responded, "We'll talk about this when we get home."

When we got home, there wasn't much discussion. The answer was, "No!" Mom didn't stop there. She contacted her brother who was a Presbyterian minister. He had a colleague, Rev. Wesley P. Walters, who had done a great deal of research into the early history of the Restoration and had published several articles critical of The Church of Jesus Christ of Latter-day Saints. Rev. Walters sent my mother some of those articles along with other pamphlets. Mom made me read a few of them to reinforce her "No!" We both thought that would be the end of my interest in the restored gospel.

The next summer my parents decided to get away for the weekend and take a trip up to Nauvoo, Illinois. They had heard about the restoration project going on up there and thought it would be a nice place for a quick getaway. We first toured the Joseph Smith properties run by the Reorganized Church of Jesus Christ of Latter Day Saints (now known as the Community of Christ). We toured the Homestead and the Mansion House. The Red Brick Store hadn't been rebuilt yet. I remember getting a drink out of Homestead's well, which at that time had a water fountain attached to it. I remember the smell of the beeswax candles they were making in the summer kitchen.

We then toured the properties owned by The Church of Jesus Christ of Latter-day Saints. I remember going to the blacksmith shop. We watched them make a horseshoe and got a prairie diamond ring. We went to the Scovil bakery and got a gingersnap. We took the horse-drawn carriage ride around the town. We also visited the Blue Cheese factory (Nauvoo was famous for its Blue Cheese at the time) and Baxter's Winery (Dad insisted on going to the winery as soon as he sampled the Blue Cheese!). It was obvious that Nauvoo was a special place. It would become a very special place to me personally and play a significant role in my conversion.

Looking back on it all, I guess you could say that joining The Church of Jesus Christ of Latter-day Saints was all my mother's fault! She introduced me to the Osmonds. She took me to the fireside, to Temple Square, to Nauvoo, and she was the one who bought our first Book of Mormon. I know you didn't want me to join, but let's face it, Mom, you started it.

After the Nauvoo trip, I would not have much interaction with The Church of Jesus Christ of Latter-day Saints (other than my random perusals of the Book of Mormon) until later in high school. But in 1983, I would have a significant encounter with Jesus Christ.

Chapter 2

Encountering Christ

I LOVED TO SING! I SANG IN SCHOOL CHORAL PROGRAMS, IN TALENT shows, and in Christmas programs. When those weren't available, I'd sing in my room, pretending to be Elvis or singing with one of the Osmonds.

During my freshman year at Alton (Illinois) High School, I participated in music classes and choir. My music teacher, Ron Kelly, took notice of me and invited me to sing in a church youth choir that he directed. It was a multi-denominational youth choir with well over a hundred kids. I was very reluctant to join at first. Even though I loved to sing, this youth choir was huge, and practices were held about an hour's drive from my home. I grew up as an only child, and though performing didn't bother me, I was pretty shy when it came to hanging around people I didn't know.

My teacher was persistent. He even came out to my house and talked to my mother about the program. My mother felt it would be good for me. She told me that I was going to at least try it out. If I didn't like it, I could quit. But I was going to try it whether I wanted to or not.

I had to fill out a questionnaire to join the choir. One of the questions asked was, "Are you a Christian?" I wrote "yes." My mother told me to change it to "no." I protested. I knew who Jesus was. I believed that He lived. Didn't that make me a Christian? Much to my confusion, my mother insisted I write "no." So, I did.

Practices began on January 7, 1983, at Parker Road Baptist Church, a Southern Baptist church in Florissant, Missouri (a suburb of St. Louis, Missouri). The practices kicked off with a retreat. That night we sang songs, played games, and had Bible study. But the moment that changed my life forever was when the church's pastor spoke to us about Jesus. He shared from scripture how we were all sinners (Romans 3:23), how Jesus suffered and died for our sins (Romans 5:8; John 3:16). He then invited us to place our faith and trust in Jesus Christ and commit our lives to Him (Romans 10:9). He invited us to pray what Evangelicals call "The Sinner's Prayer." It goes something like this—"Father in Heaven, I know that I am a sinner. I believe that Jesus Christ is your Son, that He suffered and died for my sins, and that He paid the price for my sins. I want Him to come into my life. I repent of my sins and commit my life to You. In Jesus's Name, Amen." As I pondered that invitation, it sounded like a reasonable request to me. I knew who Jesus was, and I believed in Him. But I had never committed my life to Him. It felt like the right thing to do. So, I prayed. I don't remember the exact words I used, but I prayed, and my life changed. There were no pillars of light. No theophany. But nonetheless, my life changed that night. I was a new person (2 Corinthians 5:17). This fourteen-year-old boy had his own personal encounter with Jesus Christ. Now, I *was* a Christian.

So, what was the difference? Before, I only had an intellectual understanding of Jesus. I believed that He lived, performed miracles, was crucified, and rose again. But I believed those facts in the same way that I believe that the Pilgrims sailed on the Mayflower, and that Abraham Lincoln was the sixteenth President of the United States. When I prayed, I moved beyond intellectual understanding to personal commitment. I was placing my faith in Christ. I was entering into a relationship with Him. I was making a commitment to follow Him. Intellectual understanding isn't enough to be a Christian. Even the demons "believe" in Jesus (James 2:19). You must exercise faith and make a commitment to Jesus Christ. That is what makes you a Christian.

There is a great story that illustrates this point. It's about a man who was walking a tightrope over Niagara Falls. To the delight of his audience, he made several crossings, one time even pushing a wheelbarrow. He then shouted to the crowd, "Do you believe I can push this wheelbarrow across with a person in it?" The crowd enthusiastically cheered, "Yes!" "Okay," said the tightrope walker. "Who wants to get into the wheelbarrow?" Becoming a Christian is getting into the wheelbarrow that Jesus is pushing. You're putting Him in control of your life.

The following Sunday, a friend of the family was singing in the evening worship service. I asked my mom to take me to the service. We both fell in love with the congregation. The members were so friendly. We began attending the church regularly. We even went to Sunday School!

In time, I realized the significance of the decision I had made, and I knew I needed to be baptized. On Easter Sunday, 1983, my mother and I responded to the pastor's invitation to join the church, and I asked to be baptized (my mother had previously been baptized in a Southern Baptist church when she was younger).

Before I was to be baptized, I had to meet with the pastor so he could ask me a few questions. He asked if I had committed my life to Jesus Christ and trusted Him as my Lord and Savior. I responded with, "I think so." He told me that he wanted me to be sure. So, we prayed again. I'm so thankful he did that. Many times thereafter, Satan would come and try to tell me that I didn't really know what I was doing when I made my initial commitment. But by the time I met with the pastor, we had been attending regularly for four months. I knew exactly what I was doing when I prayed in his study. That reassurance helped me ignore the adversary. The pastor went on to explain that Baptists baptize by immersion because the word "baptize" in the Bible translated to mean "to dip or immerse." I was going to go all the way under.

I was baptized on April 17, 1983. It was really cold that morning. By the time we got to church it was snowing! (Snow in April in St. Louis, Missouri is not unheard of, but it is rare.) When we arrived, one of the church leaders joked that the heater had broken in the baptistery! As if I weren't nervous enough! The baptism went well. It was still snowing when we left church. I took that as a sign. I loved snow as a kid. I believed that the Lord allowed it to snow that day. I took it as a sign of a covenant between Him and me. Every time it snows, I'm reminded of that covenant.

We continued to attend church at Parker Road Baptist and I quickly grew in my faith. A friend of mine had a study Bible with a bunch of maps and charts in the back. It was so cool. I got one for Christmas that year. That study Bible helped me gain a love for the scriptures and a desire to study them.

In time, we felt impressed to start attending another Southern Baptist church a little closer to home, and we transferred our membership to a different congregation. Again, I got involved in the youth and music programs. And I continued to grow in my faith. But soon The Church of Jesus Christ of Latter-day Saints would cross my path again.

Chapter 3

If You Can't Join 'Em, Beat 'Em

In the spring of 1984, I was listening to a late-night Christian talk show on the radio. The hosts were discussing a new book that had just been released about The Church of Jesus Christ of Latter-day Saints. Ding! A bell rang in my mind. I remember them. The book was called, *The God Makers: A Shocking Expose of What the Mormon Church Really Believes.* After listening to the program, I knew I had to get a copy of this book. The next time we visited the bookstore, I found and bought a copy.

The sensationalist writing of the *God Makers* really captured my imagination. Even though it was written by opponents of the Church, the *God Makers* reignited what would become a lifelong fascination and study of The Church of Jesus Christ of Latter-day Saints. Soon I had subscribed to every anti-Mormon newsletter that I could find.

But I didn't just read the opposing literature; I wanted to read both sides. I wrote to Church headquarters and they sent me a Book of Mormon, some pamphlets, and a book entitled, *A Marvelous Work and a Wonder* by LeGrand Richards. After I read that material, I wrote again, and they sent me a copy of *Truth Restored* by Gordon B. Hinckley and suggested I try reading *Jesus the Christ* and *The Articles of Faith* by James E. Talmage. I ordered those books and read them. By this time, I was hooked.

Studying the Restoration and history of the Church became a huge hobby for me. I began checking out books from the high school and community libraries. And I would take every opportunity I could to bash with Church missionaries.

My sophomore year in high school provided an unexpected opportunity. I was taking a communication class that required us to give speeches on and discuss the controversial topics of the day. There was one person in the class who seemed to share the same conservative viewpoint on many of the social issues that I did. She sat right next to me. She was a Latter-day Saint. While we were listening to our classmates give speeches, we passed notes back and forth. I don't think our teacher ever caught us. If he had, he would have been surprised at the content of the notes. This wasn't your typical high school student banter. These were notes of passion! We were passionately defending our faiths! These notes became theological treatises. I had to study the Church just to keep up with my classmate! But man was it fun!

Over the next few years, my Church studies would ebb and flow. I would study intensely for weeks and then put those studies aside for other pursuits. It was also during this time that I began sensing God calling me into the ministry. I remember having a conversation about this calling with my uncle, the Presbyterian minister. He gave me some great advice (though it was somewhat surprising to me at the time). "Bryan," he said, "If you can do anything else, do it."

Contrary to what some might think, pursuing a call to ministry is not for the faint of heart. Though they don't get the publicity that the TV preachers get, most ministers are ministers because God wouldn't let them do anything else.

Despite my uncle's advice, the prompting would not go away. Every night I would read my Bible and a little devotional by Billy Graham. Then I would pray. Different scriptures and devotional passages would jump out at me as I read. I can't remember specific passages, but I do remember how I felt when I read them. I really had a heart for the kids in the youth program at church. I wanted to help them. I loved music and I loved the Lord. I felt that He was calling me to go into a youth and music ministry. I had thought about becoming a missionary. I found out that one of the mission boards (the agencies that send Southern Baptist missionaries) had a department that sent missionaries out to other religious faiths, and one of those faiths was The Church of Jesus Christ of Latter-day Saints. I tried really hard to get connected with that department, but nothing really worked out. So, I decided to pursue a music and youth ministry.

Midway through my senior year in high school, I stood in front of my church and publicly declared that I felt God was calling me into the ministry. They let me know I would have their support. Though I wasn't exactly sure which direction my calling was going to take me, I knew I needed to prepare, and my first step was getting an education.

After graduating high school, I began attending Missouri Baptist College (now University) majoring in Religion. (Ironically, the St. Louis, Missouri Temple would be built right next door to, and on land once owned by, Missouri Baptist University).

While at Missouri Baptist, I took the normal courses for a Bachelor of Arts in Religion, including courses in Old and New Testament, Christian theology, and New Testament Greek. My intention at this point was to go into a youth and music ministry and maybe do a little preaching on the side. Many Southern Baptist churches have paid staff (often part time) running their youth and music ministries. I thought that would be a good fit for me. Occasionally, someone would suggest that I should consider being a pastor. But I had no desire to be a pastor.

It was at Missouri Baptist College that I wrote my first paper on The Church of Jesus Christ of Latter-day Saints. It was entitled, "Mormonism: Christian Church or Cult." It was a rehash of most of the criticisms I had read over the years. I also reconnected with my uncle's old friend Rev. Wesley Walters. We carried on a brief correspondence. He encouraged my study of the Church. I quickly gained a reputation among my friends as someone who was knowledgeable (some would say obsessed) about The Church of Jesus Christ of Latter-day Saints. People would often ask me, "Why are you so fascinated with Mormonism?" I really had no answer other than, "Why do you like to collect stamps?" I could only describe it as a weird hobby. But deep down, I felt there was something more. I could walk away from my studies of the restored Church, but the Church was always lurking there deep down. I remember there were times when I would be reading a book about some bit of Church history, and my spirit would just soar. "This was just amazing!" I would say to myself and then shake my head. "There is no way it could be true."

Around this time, I read the Book of Mormon from cover to cover for the first time. When I finished, I attempted to take up Moroni's promise and prayed as sincerely as I could. Nothing happened. Dead silence. I thought to myself, "You already know this isn't true. Why are you praying about it?" I often wondered why I got the answer I did. I've come to the conclusion that I just wasn't ready.

After studying at Missouri Baptist for two years, I transferred to Union University in Jackson, Tennessee. I continued the same course of study and graduated in June of 1990 with a Bachelor of Arts in Religion. I received a summer internship at my home church. A few months later, I would accept a position as Youth and Music Minister of North Alton Southern Baptist Church in Alton, IL.

My work as a youth and music minister was only part time, so I took another job working at a fast-food restaurant. The Lord taught me some great lessons while working at that fast-food restaurant. One of the greatest lessons was on the importance of authenticity. My best friend Chris, who also worked with me at the restaurant, and I were both Christians and wannabe musicians with long hair and the works. We were also typical twenty-year-old boys, obsessed with girls, music, ourselves, and girls. One of our co-workers, Valerie, was about ten years older than us and claimed to be an agnostic. Chris and I had many long conversations with her about faith, but we never thought anything would come of it. One morning we were greeted at work by another Christian co-worker. She was beaming. She said, "You've got to go talk to Valerie!" We found Valerie in the back. She had the biggest smile I'd ever seen. She was radiant. "Valerie," we asked. "What happened?" She went on to say that yesterday she decided to go to church. At the end of the service, the pastor invited people to accept Jesus Christ as their Savior. She said it was as if Jesus, Himself, were speaking to her. Then she said something I will never forget. She said, "I just thought about you and Chris. And I figured if Jesus could love you, He could love me too. So, I went forward and gave my life to Christ."

Brothers and sisters, people are always watching us. You don't have to be perfect, and let's face it, none of us are and many of us are faking it. People want authenticity. Valerie saw that Chris and I had an authentic relationship with Christ, warts and all. She knew she could have one, too. God is so good!

In the summer of 1992, I made another trip up to Nauvoo to watch the City of Joseph Pageant (an outdoor musical pageant that told the history of Nauvoo). I also visited Carthage Jail. In the Carthage Jail Visitors' Center, they had a book for sale called *Carthage Conspiracy*. I had read part of that book back in high school. It was really good. I wanted to get a copy, but I didn't have any extra money at the time. A few weeks later I wrote to the jail and asked if I could buy a copy of the book through the mail. A senior sister missionary wrote back telling me that I could. Sister Carol Blake and I would end up being pen pals for the next twenty years. We wrote letters and exchanged Christmas cards. Then we would send e-mails and, eventually, Facebook. We shared our faith and sent each other books and articles. Early on, Sister Blake told me that she wasn't going to give up on me until I joined the restored Church of Jesus Christ. I tried to tell her that would never happen. But she was persistent. In time, we lost touch, and I found out she was dealing with Alzheimer's. After I joined the Church, I tried desperately to get in contact with her. Eventually, I was able to get in touch with her daughter, Amy. I told her about my long correspondence with her mother and of her mother's determination to see me become a member. I wanted her to let her mother know that she had "won," that I had been baptized. Amy was able to have that conversation with her mother just a couple months before her mother passed away.

Later in 1992, I would again try to reconnect with the Interfaith Witness Department of the Southern Baptist Convention. This was that group I mentioned earlier that sent out missionaries to other faiths. They had a program at the time where you could be trained on how to share the Baptist faith with people from other faiths. If you completed the program, you could be "certified" as an "interfaith witness" to that other faith. They offered seminars on "Mormonism," but never in my area. That didn't stop me. I wanted one of those certificates badly. I eventually pestered the leaders enough that they had me write a few essays about Church history and theology and they sent me the certificate. They even allowed me to write a couple very short articles that they published in their organization's newsletter.

Over the years there were times when I tried hard to get involved in an apologetic ministry that was critical of the Church. This was the closest I ever got.

Some might ask why I wanted to be a part of such a ministry. Two reasons: 1. I needed an outlet. The only Baptists that shared my interest in the history and theology of The Church of Jesus Christ of Latter-day Saints were critics of the Church. 2. I really believed that all Latter-day Saints were going to hell. I thought they needed Jesus and I wanted to be able to share with them. Obviously, my views have changed, somewhat. Keep reading.

It was also around this time that I decided to continue my theological studies by taking extension courses through Midwestern Baptist Theological Seminary (one of the six theological seminaries overseen by the Southern Baptist Convention). For Southern Baptists, a "seminary" is a graduate school that offers master's and doctoral degrees in theological and Biblical education. After taking extension courses for a year, I felt impressed that I should continue my studies full time. I made plans to move and attend the seminary on campus.

The main campus of Midwestern Baptist Theological Seminary is in Kansas City, Missouri. There is a large cluster of Restoration Churches (churches that trace their roots back to the movement started by Joseph Smith Jr.) in the Kansas City area. It made sense that I should go there full time. I visited the campus (made my first visit to nearby Liberty Jail[1]) and moved forward with my plans. But

1. Liberty Jail was the first Church historic site I visited outside of Utah and Illinois. I remember sitting in the room circling the cutout of the jail. The lights faded and a narration began to play. I peered into the jail as the story of Joseph's incarceration was told. I remember the studded front door of the prison and being allowed to touch the barred windows. It was in this room that the opening verses of Doctrine and Covenants 121 began to speak to me. "O God, where art thou? And where is the pavilion that covereth thy hiding place?" (D&C 121:1). Who among us has not felt this way? And the words of reassurance the Prophet received . . . These verses have become some of my favorite in all the Latter-day scriptures, even before I was a member. Liberty Jail is truly, as the tour guide said, a "temple-prison." Several years later, I visited the jail while on a family vacation. I introduced myself to one of the missionaries as a Baptist pastor. I told her how much Doctrine and Covenants 121 meant to me. I'll never forget the look of shock and amazement in her eyes as I testified of the power of those verses.

then something didn't feel right. Neither I nor my mother felt a peace about me moving to Kansas City. So, I withdrew my application.

A few weeks later, we found out that my mother had cancer. Fortunately, the cancer could be treated with surgery and radiation. She was able to recover fairly quickly. When she was safely in remission, I continued my pursuit of theological education. But I still didn't feel that I was to go to Midwestern. I decided to investigate The Southern Baptist Theological Seminary in Louisville, Kentucky. I scheduled a campus visit. Before the visit ended, I knew that was where the Lord wanted me to go. I submitted my application and in January 1994, arrived in Louisville, Kentucky and moved onto campus.

Chapter 4

Saints and Southern Baptists

WITH THE START OF TERM, CAME CHAPEL SERVICE ON TUESDAYS AND Thursdays. The first chapel I attended was a "Founder's Day" convocation. The main presentation was on the life of the seminary's third president, William Heth Whitsitt. During the presentation, the speaker noted that Dr. Whitsitt had written an unpublished manuscript on the life of Sidney Rigdon. Dr. Whitsitt believed Rigdon was the "real founder of Mormonism." That got my attention. Once again, The Church of Jesus Christ of Latter-day Saints had crossed my path. I knew I had to investigate that manuscript before I left school.

My interest in the Church had been reignited. Dr. Whitsitt had amassed a huge library of books related to the Church, and those books were in the campus library. I checked them out and read as many as I could.

I soon discovered students write a lot in master's level theological work. Just about every paper I wrote had something to do with the restored Church. If there were *any* way I could relate the topic of the paper to the Church, I did.

I was still attending Southern Seminary in 1997 when they announced the open house for the St. Louis Missouri Temple. I was so excited. It would be my first experience entering a modern temple (I had only been in the Kirtland Temple at this point). I was taking a World Religions class at that time. I asked the professor if I could arrange a tour of the temple for my classmates for class credit. Southern Seminary was only about a four-hour drive from St. Louis. At that time, Church temple open houses were pretty rare. The professor agreed on the condition that the students who went on the trip would write a short paper about their experience and that I find a representative from the Church who would agree to do a Q&A with the students.

I was able to get in touch with the local leaders in charge of the temple open house. They helped me get the tour set up and put me in touch with the Church's public affairs department who agreed to provide someone to do the Q&A. The only condition is that we would have to find a location. There simply wasn't any room on the temple grounds.

No problem, I thought. Missouri Baptist College was right next door to the temple. They were a Southern Baptist college. We were a Southern Baptist seminary. Surely, they would be able to provide a room for us to have the Q&A. They refused to accommodate us. Many of the college leaders were under fire for allowing Baptist land to be sold for a Latter-day Saint temple. They did not want any "Mormons" on their campus, not even to host a Southern Baptist Q&A.

I had to scramble. The students were going to be driving from Louisville to St. Louis and back on the same day. I had to find a place close to the temple. And there weren't a lot of options that I could get for free.

Luckily, there was a Presbyterian seminary on the other side of Missouri Baptist College. My uncle (the Presbyterian minister) was an adjunct professor there. I called him and he arranged for us to have our Q&A at the Presbyterian seminary. So, there we were, a group of Southern Baptists talking with a Latter-day Saint at a Presbyterian seminary

I do not remember all that was discussed during this Q&A, but the discussion was courteous. The Public Affairs representative was a sister. She was very pleasant and forthright. The one question I do remember was on the principle of eternal marriage. One of the seminary students asked if the Church had any Biblical evidence for eternal marriage. She pointed to Adam and Eve in the Garden. She asked if we believed Adam and Eve were married before the "Fall." We agreed that they were. She then pointed out if you believe that Adam and Eve were married before the "Fall," then you must believe in marriage for eternity. For if Adam never fell then they would have been married for eternity. Latter-day Saints and other Christians have differing views on the meaning and results of the "Fall," but both groups agree that after the return of Christ and the establishment of the New Jerusalem, life on Earth will be just like it was in the Garden of Eden. If Adam and Eve were married in Eden 1.0, why couldn't others be married in Eden 2.0? It was a powerful argument; and for the first time my mind was open to the possibility of eternal marriage.

A few years later, I was able to arrange for another group of seminary students to attend the open house of the Louisville Kentucky Temple. That trip went a whole lot smoother!

It was also during my time at seminary that I met and married my wife, Jennifer. We were married on April 15, 1995. Sixteen months later, on August 17, 1996, our oldest son, Bryan Jacob "B.J." Ready was born and my GPA plummeted shortly thereafter! B.J. would be the first of our six children—B.J., Carrie, Caleb, Matthew, Kaylee, and Rebekah.

While living in Louisville, I continued to serve in the music and youth programs at different churches in Kentucky and Indiana. I also worked a part-time job with United Parcel Service.

I finally graduated with my Master of Divinity (MDiv) in Missions, Evangelism, and Church Growth in December of 1997. However, my coursework didn't allow me to really dig into Whitsitt's work. I knew I would have to go back. After taking a couple years off, I was accepted into Southern Seminary's Master of Theology (ThM) program with an emphasis on World Religions. William Heth Whitistt's unpublished manuscript would be the subject of my thesis.

Dr. William Heth Whitsitt (1841–1911) was the third president of the Southern Baptist Convention's flagship seminary, The Southern Baptist Seminary. He was a brilliant scholar whose work changed the way Baptists viewed their history. Dr. Whitsitt was also fascinated with the life of Sidney Rigdon and wrote a 1400-page biography of the early Church leader.

According to Whitsitt's biographer, W. Morgan Patterson, Whitsitt was "fascinated by the ideas, leaders, and documents of Mormonism; and by 1887, he had amassed a huge amount of information on the subject." "His curiosity about the Mormon movement seemed almost to be an obsession."[2] (I can relate!) Whitsitt did a great deal of meticulous research on this subject.

Dr. Whitsitt was the first, legitimate, non-Latter-day Saint scholar to undertake an in-depth study of the history and theology of The Church of Jesus Christ of Latter-day Saints. He undertook that study not to "expose" the church, but to understand it. Whitsitt would go on to argue that Joseph Smith Jr. was not a charlatan out to deceive. He was rather the figurehead of a group of people who felt Protestant Christianity needed a "restoration" to its apostolic roots.

During the Second Great Awakening in the early nineteenth century, there were many people who shared a belief in a needed "restoration" of the Christian church. Whitsitt argued that Sidney Rigdon felt that other groups were not going far enough. He believed a new scripture was needed to emphasize the distinctive teachings of apostolic Christianity; and new authority was needed from God to perform church ordinances. Whitsitt speculates that Rigdon had heard about Joseph Smith's treasure-seeking activities and arranged to meet with Smith as early as 1823. He argues that the Book of Mormon was the pseudepigraphal scripture, produced by Rigdon and Smith, needed to launch the work.

Most scholars today dismiss Whitsitt's theory as variation of the Spaulding-Rigdon Theory. Prior to the mid-1940s, the Spaulding-Rigdon Theory was the dominant theory (outside of the Church) regarding the origins of the Church and the Book of Mormon. The theory basically states that Sidney Rigdon had a connection to Solomon Spaulding, the author of an unpublished manuscript describing the origin of the Native Americans. It theorizes that Rigdon somehow obtained a copy of the manuscript and with Joseph Smith's help, used it as the foundation of the Book of Mormon.

---

2. W. Morgan Patterson, *William Heth Whitsitt: The Seminary's Versatile Scholar* (February 1994, Tms. Special Collections, The Southern Baptist Theological Seminary, Louisville, KY), 15.

The Spaulding-Rigdon Theory is often rejected for several reasons, including the fact that there is no evidence that Joseph Smith and Sidney Rigdon knew each other prior to December 1830; and Rigdon repeatedly stated that he'd never seen the Book of Mormon prior to October 1830 (The Book of Mormon came off the press on March 26, 1830), or had any connection with Solomon Spaulding. Even though Rigdon became disaffected from the Church, he never wavered in these assertions, even up until his death.

I spent two years working on Whitsitt. I finished my thesis entitled *William H. Whitsitt: Insights into Early Mormonism* in November 2000. I really enjoyed digging through Dr. Whitsitt's archives. There were pages and pages of notes and even some correspondence from Church leaders and early associates of Sidney Rigdon.

Though I view things much differently now than when I wrote my thesis, I still have a great deal of respect for Dr. Whitsitt's work. Whitsitt gave the Church its first scholarly look by a non-member and argued that early Church leaders were sincere men trying to initiate a restoration of apostolic Christianity. Whitsitt, obviously, did not believe Rigdon and Smith succeeded in the restoration, but he deserves our respect for his attempt at neutrality. I graduated with a ThM in December 2001.

Chapter 5

The Dark Night of the Soul[3]

While pursuing my Master of Theology degree (ThM), I was still serving as a Minister of Music and Youth at a Southern Baptist Church outside of Louisville, KY. But things were about to change. Ever since I first announced my calling to ministry, different Christians would tell me that I would be a pastor one day. I had no desire to be a pastor. I did not *want* to be a pastor. I saw some of the things that pastors had to deal with, and I wanted no part of that.

It was around 1998 that the Lord started to let me know that He was indeed calling me to pastor. I had a "Jonah" experience. I was running from the Lord's calling. I didn't literally run to a foreign land, but I dug in my heels and refused to budge. So, the Lord (figuratively) threw me into the belly of a big, old, stinky fish. I don't want to get into all the gory details, but it included some significant conflict in the church I was serving and a significant crisis of faith.

The conflict in the church boiled down to a group of people in the church who didn't like me or my wife and wanted me to be terminated from my position as the church's youth and music leader. The crisis of faith began after I heard a sermon preached by a visiting, fundamentalist preacher at the church I was attending.

3. "Dark Night of the Soul" is a poem written by a 16th century friar named St. John of the Cross. The phrase "Dark Night" or "Dark Night of the Soul" has come to describe a spiritual crisis in one's journey of faith.

For the first fifteen years of my walk with Christ, I never once doubted. I had committed my life to Jesus and that was that. I had a simple childlike faith that trusted in Jesus and His willingness to save me. But my faith would soon face a significant attack, resulting in a ten year period of doubt that I now refer to as my "Dark Night of the Soul."

This guest preacher had a very rigid view of salvation. He taught that if you didn't feel a deep sorrow for your sins, if you had never wept over your sins *before* you put your faith in Christ, then you weren't really a Christian. You couldn't be truly saved unless you felt remorse for your sins before you placed your faith in Jesus Christ. I had never heard that view expressed so strongly before. It really shook me because that was not what I experienced. When I made my decision to commit my life to Christ as a 14-year-old boy, it was a simple act of trust. I knew I had sinned. I knew I needed Jesus's Atonement to pay for my sins. But I didn't cry over my sins or feel an overwhelming power of remorse. Had I missed something? Had the past fifteen years been a fraud? I didn't believe that they were. But I really didn't know. The very foundation of my faith had been called into question.

I asked my pastor if he agreed with what the guest speaker was asserting. He said he did not agree. But since he was a guest, he didn't want to contradict him. The pastor's comments were somewhat reassuring, but I was still sinking fast. I was being sucked down into a whirlpool of doubt. I prayed and prayed and there would be moments where the Lord would whisper to me that I was indeed His. I would cry tears of relief. But it wouldn't be long until the adversary whispered seeds of doubt into my mind and I found myself drowning in the depths of doubt again. This continued for ten years—even into my tenure as a pastor. It was a terrible struggle. Here is how the Lord delivered me.

First, I went to the Bible. I could find nothing in the Bible that said weeping over your sins was a mandatory pre-requisite for salvation. Indeed, the opposite seemed to be the case— people would come to Christ in simple, childlike faith. It was only after their encounter with Christ that repentance would take place. After this study, I realized that the preacher was in error. But even that realization was not enough to pull me out of the whirlpool of doubt. You see, once the adversary plants the seeds of doubt into your mind, they spread like weeds. You think you have them all pulled up, but a few days later they have re-sprouted. To get rid of them, you must remove every seed and remove every root, and only then will you be free from the weeds that are choking your faith. It took me a while to identify and remove all the roots of these weeds of doubt.

I had another breakthrough during one of my classes in seminary. We were studying the writings of C.S. Lewis. The professor began talking about a time in his life when he was really struggling with his faith. He said he was reading Lewis's *The Screwtape Letters* and a passage really spoke to him. He read the passage to the class and it spoke to me as well. *The Screwtape Letters* is a collection of letters written by Screwtape (a senior demon in hell) to his nephew, Wormwood (a junior tempter). Screwtape gave him advice on how to trip up his subject—a young Christian. Lewis writes, in satirical form, what the Christian life must be like from the perspective of the demons who are out to tempt us. It is brilliant writing by Lewis. I highly recommend it.

In Chapter 8, Screwtape describes the Christian who is struggling with his faith. The whole chapter is filled with wonderful insight into how the Lord is working when a believer is struggling with faith. Lewis concludes this chapter with Screwtape's ominous warning:

> *Do not be deceived, Wormwood. Our cause is never more in danger than when a human, no longer desiring, but still intending, to do our Enemy's [God's] will, looks round upon a universe from which every trace of Him seems to have vanished, and asks why he has been forsaken, and still obeys.*[4]

As I heard these words, another wave of relief rushed over me. Even though I was still struggling with these doubts, my desire to believe and obey was evidence that Heavenly Father was still with me. Another weed had been removed.

Another clue to my struggle came to me one night after a long day of ministry. I had been counseling with a person who was struggling

4. Lewis, C. S. *The Screwtape Letters: and Screwtape Proposes a Toast.* (New York: HarperOne, An Imprint of HarperCollins Publishers, 2013), 40.

with life. I earnestly encouraged this person to commit their life to Christ. Later, I thought about what I said to that person. Why should I be telling another person that they should trust Christ, when I had so many doubts myself? Was I being a hypocrite? Yet deep down, I knew that was what they needed. In my heart of hearts, I truly believed that Jesus was the answer. At that moment, I realized that my faith was still there. I wasn't really doubting God. I was doubting myself. Another weed was pulled, and more importantly, I was closer to identifying the root.

I continued to read and search for the root of my doubts. Two additional books would be very helpful to me, *Morning and Evening* by Charles Spurgeon and *What Every Christian Ought to Know* by Adrian Rogers. In Spurgeon, I found a kindred soul, a pastor who struggled with doubts and insecurities, and still had a profound faith in Jesus Christ. Spurgeon was one of the most influential Baptist preachers of the nineteenth century. Adrian Rogers was one of the most influential Baptist preachers of the twentieth century. His book really helped me pinpoint the root of my problem. I can't remember the exact quote, but I found a similar quote online. Rogers wrote,

> *The devil wants to make you doubt your salvation. One of these days, he's going to say, "You say you trust Jesus. Well, just how strong is your faith? Maybe your faith is not strong enough to save you. Maybe you don't have enough faith."*
>
> *And the first thing you know, you will start examining your faith. You will gaze inside yourself, pull out your faith, and start some heavy-duty self-examination. Maybe you will begin to doubt your faith and wonder if you really have a saving faith.*
>
> *Do you know what the devil is trying to get you to do? He's trying to get you to look at your faith rather than look to Jesus. Don't put faith in faith, put faith in Jesus.*
>
> *The devil used to pull that trick on me. He used to say, "Adrian, how do you know that you really believe enough?" It shook me at first, but God taught me to turn the tables on him.*
>
> *Now I agree with the devil. I say, "You know, devil, you are right. My faith is weak, but Jesus is wonderful. I am not putting my faith in my faith. I am putting my faith in* ***Jesus****."*

> *Jesus never said, "Look at your look." He says, "Look—Come unto* ***Me****, all ye that labor and are heavy laden, and* ***I will*** *give you rest. Take* ***My*** *yoke upon you, and learn of Me; for I am meek and lowly in heart: and ye shall find rest unto your souls. For My yoke is easy, and My burden is light" (Matthew 11:28–30).*[5]

That was the root of my problem. I was not doubting Jesus or His ability to save me. I was doubting my faith. But it is not my faith that saves me. It is the object of my faith—Jesus!—that saves me. Paul taught that we are saved through faith (Ephesians 2:8), not by it. It is Jesus who saves us. And Jesus will save us even when our faith was weak. The prophet Isaiah wrote, "A bruised reed shall he not break, and the smoking flax shall he not quench" (Isaiah 42:3). Even if your faith is as fragile as a bruised reed or a smoldering wick, it is enough. It is not the quantity of your faith that matters, it is the object of your faith that matters. Didn't Jesus say that "If ye have faith as a grain of mustard seed, ye shall say unto this mountain, Remove hence to yonder place; and it shall remove; and nothing shall be impossible unto you" (Matthew 17:20)?

For a long time this verse really discouraged me. I knew I wasn't able to move any mountains, so I thought my faith wasn't very strong. But after I read Adrian Rogers quote, the verse became a strong encouragement. Jesus was telling me that even if I had the smallest amount of faith, it would be enough. Now certainly the Lord wants us, even commands us, to increase our faith, to build and strengthen our faith. But when you are struggling, it is reassuring to know that the smallest amount of faith is enough to call His aid to us.

So, there it was. After many years of doubt and struggle, I finally found the root of my problem. I wasn't doubting God. I was doubting my faith in God. That was the nasty taproot of doubt that had wedged its way into my mind. It would take several more months of digging and pulling before I was finally able to yank the whole root out. To be honest, it was more about me learning how to surrender

---

5. Rogers, Adrian. "Faith In Jesus...Not Faith In Faith." *Love Worth Finding Ministries*, April 20, 2017, www.lwf.org/daily-devotions/faith-in-jesus-not-faith-in-faith. Accessed September 18, 2020.

my doubt to God and let Him yank it out. I wouldn't have been able to do it myself.

The final tool that God used to get me to that point of surrender was a book by Dr. R.C. Sproul, *Chosen by God*. When we worry about holding on to our faith, we forget that God also has a hold of us; and He promises us that He will never let us go (John 10:28–30). In my "dark night" I was worried that I did not have a hold of God. *Chosen by God* reminded me that God still had a hold of me! Dr. Sproul had a popular radio program called "Renewing Your Mind." The program is still broadcast today. I first heard about this book on the radio program. This book reaffirmed to me that my problem was me and not God.

In the end, there was no dramatic moment where I felt the root of doubt yanked from my heart. It was a slow process; more like God sprayed some heavenly Round-Up on that weed and it finally just dissolved. I didn't give up on God and most importantly He didn't give up on me.

But Satan did not give up either. He continues to try to sow those seeds of doubt. But having gone through my struggle, I can now recognize those seeds and remove them before they have a chance to take root.

Many people struggle with doubts. Perhaps you are struggling. Let me ask you, deep down are you really doubting God or are you doubting yourself? Are you doubting your faith? Or are you doubting the object of your faith? There is a big difference. Doubting yourself is not a sin. I can say now that my faith is much stronger because I went through the struggles I did. And it was a horrible, miserable struggle, ten long years. But the Lord brought me through it; and I'm stronger for it. He will bring you through it too, just don't give up!

If you are genuinely doubting God, then let me ask you if you know Him? Was there ever a time in your life when you placed your faith in Him? Have you ever made a conscious, intentional commitment to follow Him? If not, start there. Do you want to believe? Then pray to Heavenly Father in the name of Jesus Christ and ask Him to give you faith. If you're not sure you want to believe—then pray and ask Him to give you the "want to." The story of The Church of Jesus Christ of Latter-day Saints has been woven in such a way that if you don't want to believe, you can find plenty of reasons not to believe. But! If you *do* want to believe, you can find even more reasons to believe. It boils down to what you want to do.

In concluding this discussion, let me go back to the words of that guest speaker who triggered my dark night of the soul. As I said earlier, I cannot find anywhere in the scriptures that says grieving over my sins is a prerequisite to faith in Jesus Christ. I find just the opposite. Faith in Christ precedes repentance. Indeed, we see that very clearly taught in the restored gospel. The Fourth Article of Faith states,

> *We believe that the first principles and ordinances of the Gospel are: first, Faith in the Lord Jesus Christ; second, Repentance; third, Baptism by immersion for the remission of sins; fourth, Laying on of hands for the gift of the Holy Ghost.*

Faith precedes repentance. In the intervening years, I have grieved over my sin. I have come to see what my sin cost the Savior. I know it grieves Him. I know that I deserve to go to hell. But one January night in a Baptist church in Missouri, the Holy Spirit whispered to me, and I placed my faith in Christ—my puny, bruised, smoldering, weak faith—and Jesus came into my life and promised me His salvation.

There is a story about the thief on the cross who had asked Jesus to remember him in his kingdom. The thief died and went and stood before the Lord, and the Lord asked him, "Why should I let you into my kingdom?" The thief replied, "The guy on the middle cross said I could." When I stand before God, if He asks me, "Why should I let you into my kingdom?", my response will also be, "Because the guy on the middle cross said I could."

Though the crisis of faith would continue for some time, the combination of the church conflict and my crisis of faith made me very miserable for several months. Finally, I could take it no longer and I surrendered to be a pastor.

(Note: Some of the ideas I express in this chapter regarding salvation may sound strange or even contradictory to what the restored gospel teaches. Please see my section on Salvation in the appendix for a more in-depth explanation of how these ideas fit with the teachings of the restored gospel.)

Chapter 6

Pastoring

THE WAY SOUTHERN BAPTISTS CHURCHES CALL MINISTERS IS DIFFERENT than other churches. Each Southern Baptist congregation is autonomous. Each congregation is its own 501(c)3 non-profit corporation. These churches cooperate with one another and form local associations (roughly the equivalent size of a stake). They cooperate on a national level through what is called the Southern Baptist Convention. The Convention is made up of "messengers" or representatives from each church who meet once a year at an annual meeting (similar to General Conference). At this meeting, national leaders are elected to conduct the business of the convention and run the various mission boards (responsible for sending missionaries) and the seminaries (graduate schools) sponsored by the Convention.

Each congregation is responsible for finding and calling their own pastors. In my case, when I finally surrendered to God's call to pastor, I prepared a resume and sent it to various associations and seminaries. When a congregation is seeking a pastor, they request resumes from one of those agencies. They read through and pray over those resumes. Once they identify a couple of candidates that might be a good fit for their church, they contact their references. If those check out, they will arrange for an opportunity to hear the candidate preach. If they feel the Spirit speaking during the sermon, they will invite the prospective pastor to come to the church "in view of a call." Typically, the prospective pastor will come on a Sunday morning, preach during the worship service, and there will be a potluck after church followed by a question and answer session. Afterwards, the candidate will meet with the church members who hold various leadership positions in the church.

That night, the candidate will preach during an evening service. After that service, the members have what's called a "business meeting" in which a motion will be made to call the candidate as their pastor. The motion will be discussed and then voted upon. Majority rules. If the majority of the church votes in favor, a call is extended to the candidate, and the candidate prayerfully decides to accept the call to be that church's pastor. Most pastors will not accept the call unless the voting is unanimous or near unanimous.

In October 2000, I was contacted by a representative from Mt. Zion Baptist Church in Piasa, Illinois. They told me they were looking for a new pastor. Their previous pastor had retired a few months before. They asked if I would be interested in their opening. Piasa, Illinois was only about thirty minutes from where I grew up and where my parents still lived. How they found me in Kentucky and how my resume got into their hands was a miracle! God was certainly working in this situation. I readily agreed.

On Sunday, November 19, 2000, I came to Mt. Zion Baptist Church in view of a call and went through the process I described above. When it was all said and done, the vote to call me as a pastor was nearly unanimous, only one dissenting vote. I accepted the call and started pastoring on January 1, 2001. I pastored those wonderful people for fifteen years. It would be the only church I would ever pastor.

Mt. Zion was a typical Southern Baptist church. On Sundays we would have around seventy to eighty people in attendance. Many of these folks were farmers or retired farmers. They were a great group of people.

Being a pastor of a Baptist church is similar to being a bishop of a Latter-day Saint ward in terms of ministering and leading a congregation, but there are differences as well.[6] Each church is responsible for

6. For additional information on how Southern Baptist church organization differs from The Church of Jesus Christ of Latter-day Saints, please see my article on "Baptist Polity" in the appendix.

providing and paying for their own expenses. With rare exceptions they get no financial help from other Baptist churches or the larger denomination.

My pastoral responsibilities included preaching and teaching, visiting the sick and shut-in, and general administrative oversight of the church's ministry and programs. I was an ex officio member of every committee in the church. Most Baptist churches have many committees!

I soon discovered that my strengths lay in preaching, teaching, and administrating. I would spend several hours every week in sermon preparation. I was responsible for preparing three to four sermons/lessons each week. I had to prepare and preach a twenty-five- to thirty-minute sermon on Sunday morning, another twenty-five- to thirty-minute sermon on Sunday night, and a fifteen-minute lesson for Wednesday night prayer meeting. If I was teaching Sunday School that week, I had to prepare a Sunday School lesson as well. For the Sunday School lessons there was often a pre-printed curriculum that I could use to prepare the lesson, but there were times when I simply prepared my own curriculum. There were no General Authority talks from which to prepare the sermon. Though I would occasionally borrow another pastor's sermon outline to prepare a sermon, most of the time I would get my message directly from the biblical text. Many churches wanted their pastors to have at least a rudimentary understanding of Greek and Hebrew to strengthen their understanding of the biblical text. Many pastors earned a master's degree in Theological or Biblical Studies in preparation for their church ministries, as I did. Usually on Sunday mornings, I would preach a series of sermons based upon a single book of the Bible. On Sunday evenings I would usually preach a sermon on a topic relevant to Christian living. Different pastors preach in different ways, and there is often a lot of work behind each sermon a pastor preaches.

A few months into my pastorate, the Spirit really blessed our church. We were seeing many people come to faith in Christ and we had many baptisms during those first few years. I attribute this to the prayers that were being offered by the members of the church. We had a women's prayer group that met weekly. We had a men's prayer breakfast that met monthly. And a weekly Wednesday night prayer meeting. As long as we were praying, we saw God do some powerful things. In addition to people coming to trust Jesus as their Savior, we saw people being healed.

I remember one of our church members, Betty, had been diagnosed with lung cancer. She had battled breast cancer before. So, this recurrence of the cancer was especially concerning. They had scheduled surgery to remove the tumor from her lung. The night before her surgery, I visited with her in her home. She was at peace with what she was facing the next day. She trusted in the Lord and His will.

Before I left, I prayed with Betty. I had the distinct impression that I should pray for her healing. So, I prayed and asked the Lord to heal her. There was such a power in the room at that moment.

The next day, I prepared to go visit Betty in the hospital. I called her family to see how things were going and which room she was in. Much to my surprise, Betty answered the phone. The surgery had been cancelled. She explained that when she woke up that morning, she had a bit of congestion, so the surgeon wanted a CT scan of the lung to make sure there was no pneumonia and that it would be safe to operate. The CT scan showed that the lung was free of pneumonia. But it was also free of something else. The tumor was gone! They performed additional tests to confirm that the cancer had indeed left her. It was amazing. I firmly believe that the Lord healed Betty because of the many prayers lifted on her behalf. I know that James 5:16 is true: "Confess your faults one to another, and pray one for another, that ye may be healed. The effectual fervent prayer of a righteous man availeth much."

It was fun to see the Lord at work in our church. On another occasion, I had invited another member of our congregation, Frank, to go visit a neighbor of one of our members. This person was really struggling with life. I asked her if she had ever made a commitment to Jesus Christ and if not, would she be willing to do so? She said that she was willing to try anything. I was preparing to share the gospel with this person, when the Spirit whispered, "Let Frank do it." So, I invited Frank to share the gospel with this young woman. He gave a beautiful, simple explanation. She responded by committing her life to Jesus Christ. That moment was a catalyst in Frank's life. It ignited a passion in him for sharing the gospel. He would go on to share the gospel with hundreds of people.

It was wonderful to see the Lord working in so many lives. In time, I became a passable preacher and teacher. I enjoyed both, but I was horrible at other aspects of pastoring. I mentioned earlier that preaching, teaching, and administrating were my strengths. My weaknesses were in my visiting skills. I was abysmal. One reason I was so poor at visiting is that I was (and still am) an introvert. I would much rather stay at home and read a book than go out to a party. Whereas extroverts are energized by being around groups of people, introverts are often drained after being around groups of people.

I would almost always have to take a nap on Sunday afternoons due to the combination of preaching and interacting with folks. I was drained. At that time, we also had a Sunday evening service. By the time Sunday came to an end, I was spent. Eventually, I began to spend less and less time visiting with members of my congregation at home and elsewhere. My failure to visit was one of the biggest failures of my pastoral ministry. Though my introversion was a contributing factor, I do not use it as an excuse. There are many introvert pastors who do a great job ministering to their members in their homes.

A loss of focus in my ministry was another big failure of mine. When God starts moving in a church, Satan starts moving too. Satan usually moves through people. In the first four years of my ministry, we had four families go through divorce. Now four families may not sound like much, but if you are a member of that family, it is devastating. When you are in a congregation of eighty people, four families can be anywhere from ten to twenty percent of your congregation! It had a tremendous effect on our congregation.

Furthermore, as the congregation started growing, we began to make some changes to the structure of our worship service and some of the ways we conducted business. Any time you make changes, there will be people who do not like the changes. When enough of those people start complaining, it is easy to pull your focus away from what the Lord is doing and onto the squeaky wheel. That is what I did. I got so focused on putting out these little brush fires that I forgot to focus on what the Lord was doing. It did not take long until our growth and ministry ground to a halt.

It was also during this time that our prayer ministries began to drop off. Some of the ladies in the prayer group moved away, and eventually the prayer group ended. Two of the leaders of our men's prayer breakfast moved away, and so that folded as well. Attendance at our Wednesday night prayer meeting dwindled down to me and three to four senior citizen prayer warriors. Though we still saw the Lord do many great things, the effectiveness of our overall ministry diminished.

Throughout my tenure as pastor, I continued to study the history and doctrine of The Church of Jesus Christ of Latter-day Saints. I was fortunate that Mt. Zion provided me with an office that had plenty of bookshelves. I don't know how many books I amassed. I do know that many of them pertained to the history and theology of The Church of Jesus Christ of Latter-day Saints. I dedicated two bookcases to my studies on the Restoration and soon decorated them with pictures and souvenirs from my trips to Nauvoo and visits to Latter-day Saint historic sites.

We made frequent trips to Nauvoo. It was relatively close, only about three hours away. It was quiet and peaceful, and they had plenty of free activities for the kids. We enjoyed it.

Whenever we went on family vacations, if there was a Church historic site along the way, we would stop. We stopped at Palmyra, Fayette, Harmony, Kirtland, Independence, Liberty . . . just about every major historic site from Palmyra to Nauvoo. Many times, folks would look at my library (or vacation pictures) and ask, "Why are you so interested in the Mormons?" My response was still, "I don't know. Why do some people collect stamps? It's just a weird hobby." If someone would have told me I would one day be a member of The Church of Jesus Christ of Latter-day Saints, I would never have believed them. I knew a hundred reasons why The Church of Jesus Christ of Latter-day Saints was not true.

A few years after I started pastoring at Mt. Zion. I was contacted by a Baptist congregation in Utah who wanted to know if I would be willing to come to Utah and be interviewed for their open pastorate. I jumped at the chance. I thought this would be the answer to my prayers—an opportunity to use what I had learned and actually minister to the Latter-day Saints in Utah. I was so excited, I flew to

Utah and met with the congregation there. Sadly, after the first day of two days of planned meetings, I knew it was not meant to be. The Holy Spirit made it clear to me that I would not be moving to Utah. I was devastated.

I flew back home to St. Louis with many questions swirling in my mind. I tried to get involved in ministries opposing the Church and the Lord wouldn't let me. Why? I had an opportunity to pastor in Utah and the Lord shut that door. Why? Why was I so interested in the theology and history of The Church of Jesus Christ of Latter-day Saints? Why was I spending so much time and money on something that really wasn't useful in my current ministry? It just didn't make sense. And I had no answers.

I continued to acquire books about the Restoration and subscribe to all the newsletters. Every once in a while, the missionaries would stumble upon my house. We would have a good bash and that would be the end of it. Occasionally, I would hear about something new the Church was giving away and I would order it. Then, a few weeks later, two poor, unsuspecting missionaries would be knocking on my door. I would try to be up front with them and tell them I just wanted the item. Sometimes they gave it to me and left. Sometimes they insisted on teaching a lesson and we would bash. I tried not to be mean-spirited. I honestly believed that these young men were unbelievers who desperately needed to know the real Jesus Christ.

As the internet gained popularity, I jumped online and began reading some of the various websites and blogs that popped up. I began reading the posts of those who had left the Church and noticed that most of the people who left the Church didn't become Evangelical Christians. They became agnostic or atheists. This was troubling. Most Evangelical ministries to Latter-day Saints were engaged in ministry to win the Saints to Christ. Although that was happening occasionally, it was the exception to the rule of those leaving the restored Church. It exposed a major flaw in the Evangelical to Latter-day Saint polemic, a flaw that I still see today.

Too many Evangelicals spend far too much time trying to tear down the Church and too little time lifting up Jesus Christ. I was also guilty of this mistake. The thinking is/was that if you show a Latter-day Saint the flaws of the Church, they will reject the Church and turn to Christ. That did happen occasionally, but, more often than not, when a Latter-Day Saint rejected The Church of Jesus Christ of Latter-day Saints, they rejected religion altogether, including Jesus. That was the opposite of what I wanted to happen.

As I was thinking over these things, a verse popped into my mind, "And I, if I be lifted up from the earth, will draw all men unto me" (John 12:32). I felt the Lord telling me, "Stop trying to tear down The Church of Jesus Christ of Latter-day Saints and start lifting up Jesus Christ!" I resolved to do so. I would stop bashing. I would stop talking about everything that I thought was wrong with the Church and I would start talking about everything that was right with Jesus. That moment would be a major turning point in my attitude towards The Church of Jesus Christ of Latter-day Saints.

This seems like a good place to digress for a bit and discuss the critics of the Church. Not all Church critics are the same. There seem to be three distinct types of critics: Fundamentalists, Evangelical Christians, and Former Church Members.

Fundamentalists

In talking about this group, I'm not talking about polygamists, but rather a type of Protestant Christianity that is very close-minded and self-focused. They tend to be the most bombastic of the protesters at the Church pageants and General Conference. These are the ones with the bullhorns and placards, the ones shouting in the streets. They don't just protest at General Conference; they protest at Catholic events and other Protestant Christian events. They don't just hate Latter-day Saints. They hate everyone who does not think exactly the same way they do. I once heard a fitting definition of "'Fundamentalists'—No FUN. All DAM(n), and very little MENTAL." Seems about right to me. Don't ever engage with these folks. It will do no good. "Never wrestle with a skunk. You might win the fight, but you still stink when it's over." The same can be said about engaging with Fundamentalists. For what it's worth, even the other Church critics get frustrated with these guys, especially the Evangelical group which I will move to next. They feel the Fundamentalist approach is far too confrontational, and it hinders the Evangelicals' opportunity to share with Latter-day Saints because they are often lumped in together.

Evangelicals

"Evangelical" is a term used to describe Christians from a wide range of Protestant Christian denominations who believe in the historicity and authority of the Bible and that salvation only comes by justification through faith in Christ alone. These Church critics honestly believe that members of the Church are either without Christ, or they worship a "different Christ" that cannot provide them with true salvation. These are the groups that usually just stand on the corner and hand out pamphlets or newspapers. Some will engage in a little street preaching, but they are far less confrontational than the Fundamentalists. Many of these Evangelicals pay their own way and use their own vacation time to be present at Church events in hopes that they will be able to share their faith with Church members. They do this because they are genuinely concerned about the spiritual condition of Latter-day Saints. They believe they are doing this out of love for Latter-day Saints. You may disagree, but I was in this camp for many years. Though I don't agree with their tactics anymore, I still believe that this group, for the most part, continues to do what they do out of love and a genuine concern for the Latter-day Saints' salvation.

Former Church Members

From my experience, this group can be broken down into two subgroups: 1. Former members who are mad at the Church. They feel like they were deceived and lied to and they just want to get even and warn everyone about the terrible things the Church has done! 2. Former members who have left the Church and genuinely believe they have found something better. Many of these people are in the Evangelical camp as well. Some have found peace in other faiths or no faith at all, and they want to share their experience with you.

As you encounter these groups, please remember that most of them believe their message and methods are motivated out of love and a desire to help members of the Church. If you chose to respond to these groups, please respond in love; and remember the words of that wise old rabbit, "If you can't say nothing nice, then don't say nothing at all."

I would serve as the pastor of Mt. Zion Baptist Church for fifteen years. We continued to see the Lord work. Young men were called to ministry. We helped start a church in another community. But we never saw the power that we saw during the early years of my ministry at the Church when we were of one accord and praying continuously. I cherish my time as pastor of Mt. Zion Baptist Church. They were a wonderful congregation who I still love very much.

Eventually, I would feel a pull to a different type of ministry. A ministry with members of The Church of Jesus Christ of Latter-day Saints. That story will be told in the remaining chapters of this book.

Chapter 7

My Story Goes On

IN 2004, IT WAS ANNOUNCED THAT THE "CITY OF JOSEPH" PAGEANT would end its twenty-nine-year run in Nauvoo, and a new pageant would eventually replace it. I don't think many people expected the new pageant to open the next year, but it was announced that "The Nauvoo Pageant: a Tribute to the Prophet Joseph Smith" would open the next year, in 2005, in honor of the 200th anniversary of the birth of the Prophet Joseph Smith. Out of curiosity, that summer we made the three-hour drive to Nauvoo, Illinois to see the new pageant.

The Nauvoo Pageant really stuck with me. I fell in love with it and would travel to see it just about every year. I felt a great connection with Robert Laird, one of the main characters of the pageant. His story really resonated with me for some reason. By 2011 they had developed a side production called, "Our Story Goes On" (OSGO). This show tells the story of life using vignettes and music from Broadway-style shows. I found out that OSGO would be playing at a nearby theater and wanted to go see it. I didn't want to go by myself, so I bribed my oldest daughter, Carrie, to join me, with the promise of Taco Bell afterwards.

The show was magnificent. The story, the music, everything was very moving. If you ever get a chance to see "Our Story Goes On" (it sometimes plays in Utah and occasionally in Nauvoo during pageant season), I highly recommend that you go. It is very powerful.

After the performance was over, we stayed and visited with the performers. I noticed one of the actors had a very distinct British accent. I asked him if he played "Robert Laird." He said he did. We discussed the character; and the actor, Darren Hill, discussed his experience playing the part and began sharing his testimony. Eventually, he asked the question I had been dreading, "You are LDS, aren't you?" Having studied the Church for so long, I knew "Mormonese" and could blend in pretty well. I wasn't going to lie, so I answered "No." At that moment, I felt like everything just stopped and that every head in the room just turned and looked at me. There were many missionaries in the room. Before we left, Darren had me assure him we would come up and see the pageant and then look him up afterwards.

By the time my daughter and I made it outside the theater, we were surrounded by close to a dozen missionaries. I felt like fresh meat in the Amazon being surrounded by piranha! (Okay, it wasn't really that bad, but we were definitely surrounded.) Word had gotten out that we were not Latter-day Saints. They asked me why I was there and what I thought about the program. Then they started asking me what I thought about the Church and the Book of Mormon. Now, I had bashed with scores of missionaries. I knew I could hold my own, but I also knew I was vastly outnumbered. I didn't really want to get into a major bash in front of my daughter, so I just said it was "interesting." We excused ourselves and left for Taco Bell.

A week or so later we made it back up to Nauvoo and watched the pageant. The missionaries at the pageant were offering a free CD of pageant music. To get the CD, you had to fill out a card and the CD would be "delivered" to you in a couple of weeks. I knew what that meant—missionaries! Oh well, I had dealt with them before. I really enjoyed the pageant music and wanted a copy of the CD, so I filled out the card.

After the performance, I kept my promise and looked up Darren. We had a lengthy conversation and struck up a friendship that continues to this day.

A few weeks after the pageant, I got a phone call from the missionaries asking to set up a time for them to come and deliver the CD. On Wednesday, August 10, 2011, Elders Louk and Young, along with Brother Lynn Ennis (a local ward member) showed up at my door with the CD. They gave me the CD and asked if they could share a lesson. I explained who I was and that I had met with the missionaries many times. I told them I would just be wasting their time, but they were insistent. So, we let them stay and they taught one of the missionary discussions. Now, I had bashed with missionaries so many times before, but this time was different. I would keep the promise I made to the Lord. This time I decided I would just be patient, let them say what they had to say, testify of Christ, and then end it. After all, I only wanted the CD!

After the discussion, they asked if they could come back next week and teach another lesson. I deferred again, but they continued to insist. So, we scheduled a follow-up discussion the next week. At the conclusion of the next lesson, they asked if I had any questions. Right then, a thought just hit me. It was something I had been struggling with for many years—why was I so fascinated with The Church of Jesus Christ of Latter-day Saints? I had spent so much time and money buying books and studying the Church. It didn't make any sense to me or my friends and family. Was this all a waste of time? A diabolical distraction? Or did God have a purpose in it? That was the question I wanted answered. Needless to say, we continued the discussions and then repeated the discussions.

After about three months, I was gaining a testimony about this work that I had denounced for so many years. The missionaries and Brother Ennis encouraged me to pray and ask the Lord if it were time for me to join the Church. I remember kneeling beside my bedside. I began to pour out my heart and pray. "NO," the answer reverberated in my mind. I was stunned. I thought for sure the Lord was going to say yes. When I told the missionaries, they were very disappointed. Strangely, though I had gotten a definite answer on not joining the Church, I still felt like I should continue meeting with the missionaries.

It soon became apparent that I was going to need more help than what the missionaries could provide. There are some significant theological differences between restored Christianity and historic Christianity. I needed to know if I could maintain my core theological convictions on the one hand and be a full-believing Latter-Day Saint on the other. Years ago, President Gordon B. Hinckley said, "Bring with you all that you have of good and truth which you have received from whatever source, and come and let us see if we may add to it."[7] I needed to know if his words were true. I needed help.

I wrote to the mission president, to scholars, and even to a member of the Quorum of the Twelve, who graciously maintained a brief correspondence with me. Soon it became clear to me that I needed to dialogue with a Latter-day Saint who understood historic Christian theology as well as the doctrine and history of The Church of Jesus Christ of Latter-day Saint. I had heard that Dr. Robert Millet of BYU's Religious Education Faculty had a great deal of experience with interfaith dialogue, so I wrote him and asked if he would be able to answer some questions. He graciously replied that he would enjoy that very much but was burning the candle at both ends at the present time. He indicated that he would forward my e-mail to a colleague of his named Dr. Shon Hopkin, also a member of the BYU Religion Faculty. I soon heard from Dr. Hopkin and I had my dialogue partner.

I learned a lot from Shon. We spent hours exchanging e-mails about our theological differences. One of the most important things I came to realize from my dialogue with Shon is that many Latter-day Saints professed the same passionate love and commitment to Jesus that I did. I never believed that before, probably because I had never really developed friendships with them. It became apparent to me that if I wanted Shon to accept my profession of faith in Christ as legitimate, I would need to accept his. For the first time, I could see that some (most? many?) Latter-day Saints were genuine Christians. Are all Latter-day Saints Christians? No. Are all Baptists Christians? No. Being part of an organization does not make you a Christian. What makes you a Christian is becoming a committed disciple of Jesus Christ.

Once I was able to work through some of my theological questions, it became apparent that there were three real obstacles to me joining the restored Church. I summarized them as follows: Jesus, Jennifer, and a job.

Jesus. God had called me to be a pastor. There is no way I would have ever done that job without a certainty of that calling. Since God

7. Gordon B. Hinckley, "The Marvelous Foundation of Our Faith," *Ensign*, November 2002.

had called me to be a pastor, I felt He needed to "release" me from that calling before I could leave.

Jennifer. My wife. When I told her I was thinking about resigning my pastorate and joining the Church, she was adamantly opposed to both. I could not be baptized without her consent.

Job. Though I had worked part-time jobs through most of my ministerial career, most of my income came through the church I was pastoring. I would need to find a job with which I could support my family in order to resign and join the Church.

I continued meeting weekly with the missionaries for the next year. We would take small breaks here and there, but never for more than a couple of weeks. Around Thanksgiving 2012, we decided to take another break for the holidays. Once the holidays were over, I assumed things would pick back up.

But they did not. The missionaries stopped showing up. I later found out that I had been "dropped." Apparently, some of the local church leaders and missionaries concluded that I was not making enough "progress." So, they dropped me with no phone call or explanation. It was devastating. The missionaries were my lifeline to the Church. I was still pastoring so I couldn't attend any of the meetings on Sunday mornings. The missionaries were my only real connection to the Church. And now they had dropped me cold. Luckily, Dr. Shon Hopkin, Bro. Ennis, and Don Dubree, another Church member, kept in touch with me. If they had not, I probably would not be writing this book right now.

I cannot overstate how upsetting this was. I can still feel the emotions bubbling up as I write this. They said I was not making enough "progress." But how does one measure "progress"? You see, during this period of time, Church members and missionaries were constantly urging me to "take a leap of faith"—resign the pastorate and join the Church. But when I would pray about it, the Lord kept telling me "not yet." But when I would tell the Church member or missionary what the Lord was telling me, they would simply say that "I needed to take a leap of faith." This vicious cycle continued for months. It was very frustrating. For a Church that places so much emphasis on personal revelation and agency, these folks had a hard time accepting my answers when they didn't match what they thought I should be doing.

I can see that from their perspective it didn't look like I was making progress. But I was doing my best—I was studying, I was looking for a job, I was praying and fasting. What none of us could see is what the Lord was doing.

Brothers and sisters, the Lord measures "progress" very differently than we do. The next time you are dealing with someone who doesn't appear to be making "progress," ask yourself these questions: 1. Do you feel the Spirit when you are meeting with that person? As long as you feel the Spirit, *do not stop meeting*. You don't have to meet every week. But do not drop them! 2. Is the person still praying and studying? Are they getting answers to their prayers (even if they aren't the answers you want to hear)? 3. Are you listening to the people you teach? You can't preach to them about personal revelation and then not believe them when things don't line up the way *you* think they should be. Listen to the Spirit. He will confirm the truth to you.

After about a year, we started meeting with the missionaries again about once a month. I was still in the same holding pattern—Jesus, Jennifer, and a job. Though it was a very frustrating time, we were finally all on the same page waiting on the Lord.

At one point during this frustrating period of waiting, I heard a story about a person who received a special experience with the Lord. This experience reminded her that God was with her and that He loved her. Oh, how I longed for such an experience. I prayed and asked the Lord that He would give me a sign that He loved me and that He was with me. Immediately, I was overwhelmed by a horrible feeling of sadness. A voice whispered in my ear, "Wasn't the cross enough?" In other words, "Wasn't Jesus suffering and dying for you enough to show you how much I love you?" I repented immediately.

Slowly, very slowly, things began to happen. In November 2014, I got a full-time job working for the National Archives and Records Administration's military records center in St. Louis. It didn't quite pay me enough to support my family, but things were moving in the right direction.

Six months later, the missionaries challenged me to set another baptismal date. Two baptismal dates had come and gone over the previous three and a half years. I was somewhat reluctant to set a third one. But I was willing to give it a shot. Since my father's birthday fell on a Saturday that year, I chose July 11 for my baptismal date.

My congregation had asked that I give thirty days' notice if I were going to resign. That meant I needed to resign by June 11 if I were going to baptized on July 11. I needed to figure out how I would break this to the church.

Driving home one evening, a thought came into my mind. Shon Hopkin had become a good friend of mine by now. He had spent a great deal of time dialoguing with many Evangelical Christians and knew the differences and similarities between our two churches. He knew how my church would likely react if I were to resign to become a Latter-day Saint. So, I asked him if he would write a letter to my congregation explaining how God could use me to minister to members of The Church of Jesus Christ of Latter-day Saints as a member of the Church. Shon agreed to the idea. Within a couple weeks, he e-mailed me a copy of the letter that I could read to my congregation at the appropriate time.

Sunday, June 7, 2015 was my "D-day." In order to make my baptismal date in July, I would need to resign that Sunday morning. I did a lot of praying and fasting that week. Saturday night, I sat down with my wife and told her I was thinking about resigning Sunday morning. I asked her how she felt about it. She was adamant . . . no! She did not want me to resign. I didn't understand. All the promptings I received seemed to be leading to this moment. But my wife was still opposed. Since resigning would impact the whole family, I couldn't move forward without my wife's consent. I didn't understand why this was happening, but I knew I wouldn't be resigning the next morning.

I did a lot of praying that night trying to figure out what went wrong. The next morning (Sunday), I was praying when a strange prompting came to my mind, "Read Shon's letter." "Why?" I thought. "There's no reason to read the letter. I'm not going to resign. There is no point." I dismissed the thought. We drove to church. As the family went down to Sunday School, I went to a quiet room to pray before the worship service started. Again, the prompting came, "Read Shon's letter." "No!" I exclaimed in my mind. "There is no point! I'm not resigning."

The worship service went well. The sermon seemed to go okay. After the sermon, we moved into the "Invitation" period of the service.

In most Southern Baptist churches, at the conclusion of the sermon the pastor offers an "Invitation." Now this is first and foremost an invitation to Come unto Christ. But it also offers the congregation an opportunity to pray or come and receive counseling or prayer from the pastor. Usually, the congregation sings a hymn while this is going on.

As I gave the invitation, I noticed my oldest son standing up in the back (he usually ran sound for our services). He made his way to the front of the congregation where I stood. I was pleased to see him responding to whatever spiritual prompting he was receiving. But what he said to me almost floored me. He came up to me and whispered in my ear, "Dad, the Holy Spirit just told me to tell you that you need to read Shon's letter!" I was stunned! Later my son told me that the prompting was so strong that he felt he was going to be physically sick if he didn't come and tell me to read the letter. Well, needless to say, I finally got the message about reading the letter. I didn't read the parts about resigning, because the Lord had not yet given that peace to my wife. But I read the parts about how I could be a useful minister among members of The Church of Jesus Christ of Latter-day Saints.

Below is the full text of Shon's letter/email.

Dear friends in Christ,

I'm writing this short email to ask and encourage you to continue your love, friendship, and support for Bryan as he discusses with you his decision to join the LDS church. I'm sure that in many, many ways this seems like a horrifying decision, and might cause you to believe that you no longer know Bryan or can no longer trust him.

I have been in dialogue with Bryan for two years, and during the time we have gotten to know each other, Bryan has presented Reformed/Baptist doctrine with clarity, with strength, and with conviction. The Bryan I know is fully committed to the sovereignty of God, to the substitutionary atonement of Jesus Christ, and to the belief that salvation comes by the grace of Christ alone through faith in his power to save. I believe that these convictions, centered in Christ, burn brightly and deeply in Bryan's heart, mind, and soul, and that these central beliefs will always define him, guide him, and protect him from any type of "bad theology" no matter what its source. I have been deeply impacted by Bryan's witness to me and his ability to clearly explain his beliefs. I am not the same person or the same Christian that I was before the dialogue with Bryan.

I speak as a committed Latter-day Saint when I say that I don't believe Bryan will need to give any of those central convictions up to become LDS. If he thought that were the case, he would never do it (and I wouldn't want him to). If he ever becomes convinced that those central convictions are incompatible with life as a Mormon, I'm confident that he will leave. I'm also confident that Bryan can have a powerful impact on the Latter-day Saints with whom he associates. In that sense, you might say that God can do more with Bryan inside the fold as a Latter-day Saint as he tries to draw souls to Christ than he has been able to do with him outside the fold. Bryan will be a powerful advocate for Jesus Christ, today and always, no matter what community he is in, and I believe this is one of the reasons God is calling him to join the LDS church. As a committed Latter-day Saint, one who was raised to believe in the centrality and absolute necessity of Jesus in order for mankind to be saved, I believe there are also many other reasons that Bryan feels drawn to the faith. But his witness of Christ will always be of greatest importance to him.

Bryan has mentioned to me that leaving his Baptist congregation is one of the greatest challenges for him in joining the LDS church. He loves you dearly and believes that Jesus called him to lead you, but that Jesus is now calling him along a different path. I hope that you will not feel that he needs to sever ties completely. In all of the most important ways, Bryan is still the same soul that you have always known. I hope you'll be able to catch a glimpse of just how much good he can do in this way.

Warm regards,
Shon Hopkin
Professor of Religious Education
Brigham Young University

Afterwards, I told the missionaries that I felt really bad about my baptism falling through, again! One of the missionaries, Elder Fullmer, reassured me that I shouldn't feel bad. He said that setting the date was a way of being stretched. Setting the date was not in vain. It was a way that the Lord was stretching me and stretching my faith. He was right!

At the time, I didn't understand why the Lord wanted me to read the letter. But looking back, I can see that reading the letter helped stimulate a discussion between my congregation and me about my desire to minister to members of The Church of Jesus Christ of Latter-day Saints. That helped prepare my congregation for the time that I would resign. Over the next few months, we would have many conversations, both formal and informal, about my desire to minister among and with members of The Church of Jesus Christ of Latter-day Saints.

As the October 2015 General Conference approached, I was still confused, even downright frustrated as to why things hadn't moved forward. I prayed that I would get answers from Conference. I was not able to watch all the talks live, so I downloaded them and listened to them while I was working. On the Tuesday following Conference, I listened to the talks given by Elder Neil L. Anderson and Elder Randall K. Bennet. They were both on the subject of faith. I wondered if I were being prompted to finally take that leap of faith and resign. The following Wednesday night would have been an appropriate time to resign. It was the occasion of our congregation's bimonthly business meeting. Most Southern Baptist churches periodically have what they call "Business Meetings." It's a time when the congregation gathers to discuss the "business" (such as church budget, expenditures, new policies, and personnel decisions) of the church.

I fasted all day Wednesday and prayed as often as I could. It was a day filled with anxiety. Finally, I just prayed that God's will would be done at the business meeting. Long story short, I did not resign that night.

The next day I was listening to the talk given by Elder Von Keetch (then of the Seventy) entitled, "Blessed and Happy are Those Who Keep the Commandments of God." His talk really hit home for me. He was reminding us that "the barriers established by the Lord create for us a safe harbor from evil and destructive influences." In making this point, he told a story about a visit to Australia. While walking along a beach in Australia he encountered some surfers who were upset about a barrier that had been erected at the mouth of the bay leading to the beach. The surfers were frustrated that they had come all the way to Australia to surf these famous waves, but the barrier was preventing them. It wasn't until an older man pointed out the sharks on the other side of the barrier that they could finally understand why it was there. "'Don't be too critical of the barrier,' he [the older man] said. "It's the only thing that's keeping you from being devoured.'"

Elder Keetch went on to say,

> *As we stood on that beautiful beach, our perspective had suddenly changed. A barrier that had seemed rigid and restrictive—that seemed to curtail the fun and excitement of riding the really big waves—had become something very different. With our new understanding of the danger that lurked just below the surface, the barrier now offered protection, safety, and peace.*
>
> *As you and I walk the paths of life and pursue our dreams, God's commands and standards—like the barrier—can sometimes be difficult to understand. They may appear rigid and unyielding, blocking a path that looks fun and exciting and that is being followed by so many others. As the Apostle Paul described, "We see through a glass, darkly" (1 Corinthians 13:12) with such a limited perspective that we often cannot comprehend the great dangers hidden just below the surface.*
>
> *But He who "comprehend[s] all things" (D&C 88:6) knows exactly where those dangers lie. He gives us divine direction, through His commands and loving guidance, so that we may avoid the dangers—so that we may set a course in our lives that is protected from spiritual predators and the gaping jaws of sin.*[8]

That struck me like a ton of bricks. There were things going on behind the scenes that I didn't know about, unseen dangers and problems that needed to be resolved before I could move forward. The Lord was working on those things and I just needed to be patient. I had my answer and I felt peace. A great burden was lifted off my shoulders. You see, it wasn't just my own impatience that I had been dealing with. I was still dealing with the pressure of well-meaning church members who kept insisting that all I needed to do was "take

8. Von G. Keetch, "Blessed and Happy Are Those Who Keep the Commandments of God," *Ensign*, November 2015.

a leap of faith" and all would be well. But the Lord kept telling me to wait. Some members were openly scoffing at the idea that I would ever be baptized. They called me an "Eternal Investigator." After all, it had been four years since I started this process. But the answer I received at General Conference quelled all that confusion. I was at peace and content to wait as long as the Lord wanted me to wait.

Turns out, I didn't have to wait long. It was as if the Lord needed me to learn that lesson in order for things to move forward. And once I learned that lesson, things started moving, quickly!

The very next Sunday I was preaching a message on the Tower of Babel (Genesis 11:1–9). After the Great Flood, the Lord told the people to scatter and replenish the Earth. But they didn't scatter, they stayed in one place. So, the Lord scattered them by confusing the languages. As I was preaching on this text, a voice *exploded* in my head, "*Go! I told you to go. Now, GO!*" Normally the Spirit whispers to us in that still, small voice (1 Kings 19:12), but on occasion, He shouts. This was one of those times when He shouted. It was the same voice that had told me "no" four years earlier. The voice struck me with such force that I felt like I couldn't breathe. The words continued to reverberate in my head. I was still preaching. I could hear words coming out of my mouth, but I have no idea what they were. Evidently, they made sense because no one seemed to notice what was going on. I knew in that moment that the Lord was telling me it was time to resign. It was time to go. He wasn't telling me to be baptized, yet, but I had just received clear instruction it was time to "Go." Jesus had just released me from my calling. But how was I going to tell my wife.

Jennifer and I had not discussed my resignation since that Saturday night in June. As far as I knew, she was still vehemently opposed. But I knew I had to move forward. How could I explain this to her? I commenced a week of praying and fasting. The following Saturday, I summoned up my courage and broke the news to her. We were in the car when I told her what had happened. I told her I had been fasting and praying for a week. I believed the Lord was telling me it was time to resign. I then steeled myself for her reaction. "You should have told me earlier," she said, "I could have saved you a week of fasting. The Lord told me last Friday that you were going to resign, and everything would be alright."

If I hadn't been driving the car, I think I would have fainted. I asked her when this happened. She was cleaning the kitchen and a voice just came to her and told her I was going to resign, but everything would be alright. God had told her I was going to resign before He told me! The Lord certainly works in mysterious ways.

Now, how was I going to deliver the news to my congregation? I really wanted all the key leadership and as many members as possible to hear the news from my own mouth, rather than through the grapevine. Due to the different ministries our congregation was involved with on Sunday mornings, it was rare for all our leaders to be present in the same service. I prayed that the Lord would give me wisdom in the timing of all of this.

Miraculously, the next morning most of our members and all of our key leadership were present during the morning service. That Sunday, October 18, 2015, I announced my resignation. I told them that I would stay through the end of the year. It's really rough on a congregation not to have a pastor during the holidays. I didn't want to put my congregation through that. I felt peace about staying through the end of the year. Interestingly enough, that Sunday I was preaching on the call of Abraham in Genesis 12. It was the perfect scripture for that day.

The congregation reacted as I expected. Some were upset that I was leaving (I'm sure a few were happy as well!). But because of what was set in motion last June, most understood why I was resigning and understood I felt it was a calling from the Lord.

Six weeks later, I received a promotion and pay-raise at The National Archives. Things would be very tight. But with the Lord's help we would make it financially.

Sunday, December 27, 2015, was my last Sunday as their pastor. I had served exactly fifteen years as their pastor. My last official ordinance in the Southern Baptist church was baptizing my daughter Kaylee as a follower of Christ.

The next Sunday, I attended the fast and testimony meeting at the Alton Ward of The Church of Jesus Christ of Latter-day Saints, and I bore my testimony of the Church and the Lord's timing. As part of my testimony, I confessed the critical spirit that I had toward the Church for most of my life and asked for forgiveness.

Jesus had released me from my calling as a pastor. He had spoken to my wife and let her know things would be alright. He had given me a Job which would support my family. I hadn't been baptized yet. But I had just taken a huge leap of faith. I had done what various members of the church had been telling me to do for the past four years. But had I done it any earlier, it would have been a complete disaster. I had to wait for the Lord to tell me to "jump." When He did, I jumped, and the Lord had everything in place to catch me.

Life soon began feeling normal again. I missed the people from my previous congregation, and I really missed preaching (still do). But I had a peace about my decision to resign. I attended ward meetings regularly. It was different, and it took me a while to get used to it. There was no sermon, but a series of "talks" given by ward members. The hymns, though beautiful, were so slow! Even the more jubilant ones could sometimes mimic the speed of a funeral dirge. When I prayed, I was asked to pray using formal, King James English. It was hard. Instead of focusing on what I wanted to ask the Lord, I had to focus on using Thee, Thou, and Thine in place of You and Yours (I still struggle with this).

Occasionally, members would still question me about baptism. But for the most part, they realized my resignation proved I was serious about the Restoration. I really couldn't have moved forward with baptism had I wanted to, because my wife, though she reluctantly agreed for me to attend services at Church, did *not* want me to be baptized. The local Church leaders would not allow me to be baptized without her consent.

I still prayed (and occasionally fasted) about baptism, but I was at another dead end. Without my wife's consent, I couldn't be baptized. So, I didn't focus on it too much. I remembered my lesson on patience from Elder Keetch's message.

Things began to change around April when Shon let me know he would be in town for a few days on a business trip. He wanted to know if we could get together. A thought dawned on me—wouldn't it be cool if Shon could be the one to baptize me? He wasn't coming into town until the end of June, so it could be possible. I told Shon to pack some white clothing just in case! I only told Brother Ennis what I had in mind. I didn't want people to get their hopes up if a fourth baptismal date came and went. No one else in the ward knew about the potential date.

Chapter 8

Baptism

As the dates of Shon's arrival drew nearer, I prayed and fasted more frequently. I continued to bring up the subject with my wife and she continued to object. Shon would be in town for just about three days. He was arriving on Monday, June 20 and flying out on Thursday, June 23, 2016. I tentatively set Wednesday, June 22 as the baptismal date. Again, the only two people who knew this was a possibility was Lynn and Shon.

A week out, I broke the news to the missionaries. They became very excited! I told them I had still not received permission from my wife, but I would like to go ahead and schedule the baptismal interview with the zone leaders (our district leader was one of the missionaries in our ward). I wanted to get all my ducks in a row, because if things were going to happen, they were going to happen fast. The missionaries told me that we could not do the baptismal interview until I received my wife's consent. I was disappointed but trusted that the Lord would work everything out. The next day I got a phone call from the zone leaders saying that they were going to be in the area that evening and wanted to know if I could meet for the baptismal interview! They were short on miles! I agreed.

With that out of the way, the only thing left was to obtain my wife's consent. I decided to write her a letter. I wrote about what was on my heart, what I felt God was calling me to do, and asked for her permission to be baptized. On Friday night I placed the letter on her dresser where she would see it. There were less than five days remaining until the scheduled baptism.

Monday afternoon, Shon was in town! We met after I got off work and went out to eat. We had a great visit. He asked if things were still on for Wednesday. I said, "Yes, tentatively." We agreed to get together again even if the baptism didn't work out.

After supper, I dropped Shon off at his hotel room and drove home. On the drive home, I had a very strong prompting to pray for my wife and pray for the letter I had written to her. All the way home, it kept hitting me over and over again, "Pray for your wife. Pray for the letter." When I arrived home, I noticed that the letter was sitting on my dresser. I tucked it away and resolved to read it in the morning before I went to work.

When I opened my letter the next morning, I noticed that my wife had written a short note at the bottom of the letter. "If you really feel this is what God wants you to do, then I won't stop you." It wasn't exactly permission. But it was enough. I called Brother Ennis and told him what the note said. He agreed that was all we needed. Plans were set in motion for the baptism and word spread quickly. I texted the missionaries, "Houston, we are 'go' for launch."

When I called Brother Ennis that morning, only five people knew I was getting baptized: Brother Ennis, Shon, my oldest son Bryan Jacob, my wife Jennifer, and another good Latter-day Saint friend, Don Dubree. The rest of my family did not know. I thought it would be best if I just went ahead with the baptism and then explained things to the rest of the family later. Tuesday evening, my daughter Carrie came bursting into my room ranting about a Facebook post by a well-meaning member congratulating me on my decision to be baptized! I was in trouble! I immediately called my friends, thanked them for their encouragement, explained the situation, and asked them to please delete the post, since I hadn't told anyone about the baptism yet. I then explained to my family that I had planned to tell them Thursday, after everything was done. The phrase "I was going to tell you Thursday" has now become a comical catchphrase in our household. Anytime someone neglects to tell someone something, the response is usually, "Oh, I was going to tell you Thursday."

In the end, it all worked out for the best. Carrie would be the only member of my family to attend my baptism. The other family members had their reasons for not going and I respected those reasons. But I must say, it was nice having my daughter there.

The baptism itself was typical. Shon immersed me in the water and that was that. It was a beautiful symbol of the death, burial, and resurrection of Jesus Christ.

After the service, the bishop gave me some great advice. They were going to wait until Sunday for my confirmation and the gift of the Holy Ghost. The bishop said that because of the delay, I was going to be vulnerable. He warned me that Satan would attack me. He would make me doubt my decisions. Man, am I ever glad he gave me that advice. The next morning, I was miserable. Doubts and depression flooded my soul. The bishop told me to call him if I needed to talk. I did. He told me just to hang on until Sunday. They were four of the longest days of my life.

Sunday morning, June 26, Brother Lynn Ennis confirmed me a member of The Church of Jesus Christ of Latter-day Saints. The thing I remember most about this ordinance was the "weight." The weight of the men's hands on my head during the ordinance, and the complete release of all weight when the ordinance was completed. The doubts and depression left immediately. I was now a member of The Church of Jesus Christ of Latter-day Saints. Who would have imagined that?

Immediately after I was baptized, my daughter asked, "Dad, can we be in the Nauvoo Pageant?" Carrie and Caleb really loved the pageant and wanted to participate. I told them we could apply and see what happens. Just over a year later, we were participating in the Nauvoo Pageant as part of the family cast. To kick off the pageant, the core cast performed "Our Story Goes On." My daughter and I were in the audience watching the show. We had come full circle.

Chapter 9

The Nauvoo Pageant

The Nauvoo Pageant is an experience like no other. You park in an open field across from the pageant grounds. At the entrance to the pageant, you find a country fair laid out before you. You see bagpipers, period games, crafts, and stick pull. You can learn how to dance period dances with a live band. There is even a tent where you can log onto a website and see if you were related to any of the characters in the Nauvoo Pageant.

The pageant is narrated by Parley P. Pratt. He tells the story of how, in a space of about seven years, Nauvoo became the home of The Church of Jesus Christ of Latter-day Saints, grew to be one of the largest cities in Illinois, and was largely abandoned by her citizens who left to escape persecution and find a new home in the West.

The pageant weaves the lives of Church leaders such as Joseph Smith, Brigham Young, Eliza Snow, and Jane Manning with fictional characters such as Robert and Becky Laird and Twizzleton Turley. As I mentioned earlier, Robert Laird was one of my favorite characters. He reluctantly leaves England and comes to Nauvoo, pulled in the wake of his member wife Becky. Along the way, Robert experiences a great tragedy and develops a great animosity toward the Church and the Prophet Joseph. But as he stays in Nauvoo, he begins to work on the Nauvoo temple and finds healing. In the penultimate moment, Robert and Becky enter the temple in Nauvoo, calling it "the Highlands of Heaven."

The Nauvoo Pageant has a core cast of about 20 professional actors who play the main characters. An additional 150 volunteers play the townspeople of Nauvoo. And there are an additional 100–200 people who work behind the scenes or run the Country Fair that precedes the pageant each night. I quickly fell in love with this pageant and went to see it just about every year.

In 2014, the British Pageant opened in Nauvoo. The British Pageant tells the other side of the story. It tells the story of the British Saints, starting with the British Reformers such as Tyndale and Knox, all the way down to 1837, when Heber C. Kimball arrived in Preston, England to open the British Mission. It tells of the work in the British Isles and the sacrifices those saints made to come to Nauvoo. It is a wonderful sister to the Nauvoo Pageant. Together they tell the story of the Saints in Britain and Nauvoo like corresponding stanzas in a lovely rhyme; and like a good rhyme, the pageants run on alternating nights.

A few weeks after I was baptized in 2016, we went up to watch the pageant again. I had a friend that was volunteering in the pageant that year. She introduced me to the pageant president, President Ricks, and told him a little bit about my story. President Ricks invited me to bear my testimony at one of the cast meetings held prior to the performance. It was a great thrill to be able to share how much the pageant meant to me and the role it played in my conversion.

Now that I was a member, two of my kids, Carrie and Caleb, really wanted to be in the pageant, so we applied to be in the family cast. The family cast are those volunteers who play the role of the citizens in Nauvoo. The application process begins in September of the previous year. You go online to Nauvoopageant.net and fill out an application. Eventually, you will also need to submit medical paperwork affirming you are healthy enough to participate, and a bishop's endorsement affirming your willingness to follow Church standards. This information is then prayerfully reviewed by those responsible for casting the pageant. So, we submitted our application and paperwork, and began the wait.

The weekend before Christmas 2016, I received the e-mail from the pageant secretary telling me that we had been accepted into the 2017 Nauvoo Pageant. When I showed the e-mail to my daughter Carrie, she began to scream! But I told her she had to be quiet, because it was early in the morning and I didn't want the whole house to wake up! It was funny watching Carrie trying to contain her excitement without waking up the house. The expression on her face is one I won't forget.

We had been called to serve in the Red Cast of the Nauvoo Pageant. Each family that volunteers for the family cast is normally assigned to serve in a cast for two weeks. There are five casts that cover the pageant season: Red, Blue, Yellow, Green, and Gold (the Gold cast only serves for one week). You spend the first week in Nauvoo rehearsing. The second week you perform the pageant at night and help the incoming cast with rehearsals during the day. You also have more free time to sightsee during the second week.

Now that we had been accepted into the pageant, our first task was to find housing. After Christmas, I was able to arrange for us to stay in a "tiny house" at a campground near Nauvoo. Next, we had to find shoes to go with our costumes. They had to look like shoes from the time period but be comfortable enough to wear on stage for long periods of time. Family cast members are responsible for paying their own way to Nauvoo, including food and housing while staying in Nauvoo. The pageant provides the costumes.

In February, we received an information packet about the pageant. This contained the music and words of the songs we had to learn. Learning the lyrics for the Nauvoo pageant was easy because we'd heard them so many times. Learning the lyrics to the British pageant was much more difficult. One of the songs was sung in the Welsh language. I don't know if I ever got the hang of that one, but the meaning of those lyrics was beautiful. This song is sung as the Welsh Saints are preparing to leave their homeland and sail to Nauvoo. I think it beautifully captures what must have been in their hearts as they left. A rough translation is as follows:

Fear you not, Life's experiences
Jesus, Jesus with you
Don't forget the Spirit's impression
As you leave the Land of your Fathers
Beautiful Savior, I now worship
It is thou who will take me to that shore

Longing for Wales,
Longing for Jesus
All my lifetime now in His love.

(translation provided courtesy of Nauvoo/British Pageant Staff)

Over the next few months, we would get occasional e-mails with information to help us prepare for the pageant both spiritually and temporally. In February, I got an unexpected blessing—we were going to get a larger than expected tax return! When I applied for the pageant, I was not sure how I was going to pay for everything. The additional tax return was large enough to cover almost all of our planned expenses.

Sunday, July 2, 2017 was the day we were told to report to Nauvoo. We left just after church. Our first stop was the campground and site of our "tiny house." We went to the office, but there was no one there. Finally, we were able to locate one of the site hosts who was out mowing and they sent someone to check us in. When all was said and done, the price for our housing was almost double what I had expected! I had no idea how I was going to pay for it all. Fortunately, the manager was willing to let us pay for a couple of days at a time. Miraculously, on Tuesday my state income tax return came in, and we had enough money to pay for the rest of our stay.

The "tiny house" we stayed in was nothing more than a wood storage shed with plumbing and some beds. It had a tin roof that sounded like you were in the middle of snare drum when it rained. It smelled like the lumber department of Home Depot. (Normally I like the smell of Home Depot's lumber department, but I wouldn't want to live there.) It had no insulation, just bare wood studs and the outer-plywood walls, and a small air conditioner.

After we stowed are stuff into our "tiny house," we went over to the Pageant Headquarters (PHQ) for our costume fitting. The PHQ is about a mile east of town. It is a large building that houses costuming, a rehearsal hall, pageant offices, and a small cafeteria. It also serves as the site of the sacrament meeting for the pageant cast while in Nauvoo.

For costume fitting you are greeted by one of the sisters in the costume department. They look up your name on a list to determine what part in Nauvoo Society you have been assigned to play. The possibilities range anywhere from "ruffian" to "farmer" to "merchant." You are then given costumes that correspond to your "class." The sister walks you through rows of costumes and picks out the outfits that come closest to your size for both the Nauvoo and British Pageants. You then take those costumes and go into a changing room to try them on. If they are too long, you will be taken over to another group of sisters who pin the costumes to be hemmed. Then you put your regular clothes back on. You take the costumes that are ready to go with you. The rest will be hemmed by the sisters and given to you later. After costuming, you go to the hair salon, where you will be taught how to wear your hair for the performance. For the men, it is pretty basic—as scruffy as you want it with no parts in your hair. For the women it is much more complicated with braids, and parts, and bonnets, etc.

After we finished with hair, we went to eat in the cafeteria. Prior to the start of pageant, we were given the option to sign up and pay for a cafeteria plan. I knew we would not have time to eat Sunday night, so I purchased dinner for Sunday evening and lunch for the rest of the two weeks we would be in Nauvoo. That worked out well for my family.

After we ate, we went to the rehearsal hall and sat in the bleachers that lined the north side of the wall. It was time for our orientation to begin. We were introduced to the Pageant Presidency, the Core Cast members, and directors. We were given an overview of what to expect for the next two weeks.

I must admit, at this point I was pretty overwhelmed. I had not realized what I was getting myself into, and I was still really stressed about how we were going to pay for housing.

After the meeting, we went and watched the Core Cast perform "Our Story Goes On" on the pageant stage. It was a powerful moment for me. Sitting there watching it with my daughter Carrie brought back powerful memories of her and me watching it five years ago in Edwardsville. I had come full circle.

After the performance, we went back to our "tiny house," took showers, and went to bed. We had to report for rehearsal at the pageant stage at 8:00 a.m.

We arrived at the stage, just before 8:00 a.m. the next morning. We slathered sunscreen and bug spray over our arms, necks, and faces. It was going to be a typical July day in Nauvoo, very hot and humid.

Thankfully, the pageant directors did not observe Mormon Standard Time. They started promptly at 8:00 a.m. They opened with prayer, made a few announcements, and then we hit the stage for rehearsal. We rehearsed until 10:00 a.m. when we broke for "District Meetings" in the nearby grove. District Meeting would soon become one of my favorite parts of the pageant.

Every family is assigned to a "district" while serving in a pageant. The district is named after one of the streets in Nauvoo. We served in the "Wells"[9] district with the Palmer Family. We really grew to love the Palmers—John and Natalie and their children, Brielle, Brooklyn, Blaire, and Braden. Our district leader was Hannah Cutler, she was a member of the Core Cast and she played Eliza R. Snow in the pageant. The district you are assigned to really determines everything about your participation in the pageant. It determines your "class" and costume, the scenes you are in, what props you use, and your staging in the show itself.

For District Meeting, you sat down in the shade, had a little snack, and your district leader (a member of the Core Cast) would share a spiritual thought. Later, the director would come in and apply some spiritual principles to the parts we were rehearsing that day.

After break, we were back on stage rehearsing till noon when we would break for lunch.

Carrie, Caleb, and I drove back to PHQ to eat in the cafeteria. Since the air conditioner in our "tiny house" didn't work that great in the daytime, we opted to take naps on the bleachers after lunch until it was time for dance rehearsal.

Now officially we do not dance in the pageant. We "move with joy." But it sure looked like dancing to me; and I hated dancing, largely because I'm not very good at it. I have no rhythm below my

9. During our stay in Nauvoo, we visited the Land and Records Office to do a little research. Though I did not have any direct ancestors who were members of the Church, I knew I had some distant cousins who were members during the Nauvoo period. I discovered that some of them actually lived in the Wells district of Nauvoo!

knees. Dancing was the absolute worse part of the pageant for me. My kids loved it though and they would try to help me learn the steps. Our choreographer, Stacia Hardy, saw my plight and offered to give remedial dance lessons during our lunch break. It meant fewer naps, but I was starting to get the hang of things. I felt a little better when other people started joining us in our remedial dance lessons.

Dance rehearsal for the family cast lasted from 2:00 p.m. to 4:00 p.m. Then we would break for supper. The kids and I went back to our "tiny house" and ate lunchables. That's really all we needed. You get a good meal for lunch and we were so tired and hot, we preferred sleeping rather than eating. We reported back to the pageant stage at 6:00 p.m. We rehearsed until 10:00 p.m. After some last-minute announcements, we went back to our rooms, showered, and went to sleep.

That is what the first week in Nauvoo is like, rehearsing from 8:00 a.m. to 10:00 p.m. every day. On Wednesday we actually had to be there at 7:00 a.m. to learn how to "build the temple" (the building of the Nauvoo temple is one of the central themes of the Nauvoo Pageant. The temple is built and razed on stage every night of the Nauvoo Pageant). It is a grueling schedule. I have never sweated so much as I did in Nauvoo. There were nights when I would take a shower just to dry off. It was intense. Every spare moment you could find to sleep, you spent sleeping. I never looked forward to a Sabbath day as much as I did for that next Sunday. I could not believe I was spending that much money and two weeks of my vacation time for this self-inflicted torture.

The kids, however, were having the time of their lives. They loved the dancing and the music and the other kids. Carrie was picked to be one of the "street-throwers." There is a scene where the Prophet is instructing Hyrum on how he wants the city of Nauvoo to be laid out. As he mentions the name of a street, a colorful ribbon of fabric is thrown up into the air and spread out across the stage representing that street. Carrie was one of those who threw the ribbon/street up into the air.

Caleb was disappointed when he didn't get picked to be a street thrower. That disappointment was short lived when one of the directors pulled him aside and asked him if he wanted to play the role of Brigham Young's son. "Yes!" he exclaimed. He thoroughly enjoyed working with the actors who played Brigham and Mary Ann Young (Ken Ekloff and Denise Williams). After a few days, both Carrie and Caleb relayed to me that they had made more friends in the few days they had been in Nauvoo, than all their years in school. They were having a blast. I felt like I was going to die!

Finally, Sunday arrived! We went to sacrament meeting. After eating lunch in the pageant cafeteria, we did a little sightseeing. We took Carrie's picture next to the Granger street sign (that was the name of the street she was "throwing"), we took Caleb's picture in front of his "home" (Brigham Young's home), and we took a nice nap.

Monday morning, we reported to the pageant stage at 8:00 a.m. We would be practicing our dance choreography on the stage. The pageant stage is slanted and has many lips and uneven surfaces. It has claimed many a twisted ankle. We had just finished rehearsal for one tricky dance that ends with us walking in a pinwheel shape across the stage. I was preparing to exit upstage, when I heard the director say my name, "Brother Ready," over the loudspeaker. I turned and looked at the foot of the stage where I saw a crowd of people who were surrounding my daughter who was lying down on the foot of the stage. She had hurt her ankle pretty badly. It was obvious that she was in a lot of pain. I did not know if she had broken it or not, and with the heat and humidity, I was worried that she might go into shock. I asked for someone to give her a priesthood blessing (I had the Melchizedek Priesthood at this time, but I had never given a blessing before. I was too nervous to try to do it myself). There were some brethren standing nearby, and one of them had consecrated oil. They asked who I wanted to give the blessing. I just picked two brethren at random. We had the blessing. Then the miracles started happening.

No, Carrie wasn't healed right away. But the EMT's came and splinted Carrie's ankle. They didn't think it was broken, but they wanted us to get an x-ray just in case. The Palmers took Caleb with them to their place while we took Carrie to the Emergency Room. A member of the Core Cast had just been to the hospital last week (for another sprained ankle). They rode with us and showed us how to get to the hospital. We made it to the emergency room. The x-ray was negative. The doctors at Ft. Madison (Iowa) Community Hospital were just as nice as they could be. They gave Carrie a splint and crutches.

We were in and out of the emergency room in less than an hour! Fortunately, there was not a lot of damage to the ankle itself but there was a lot of swelling. She was told that she could do whatever she could tolerate. But it was unlikely that she would be able to perform the following night. Carrie was devastated.

When we made it back to the rehearsal that night, we found out that there were not just one but two physical therapists serving in the cast that week (another miracle). They both showed Carrie some exercises and tips that would help her ankle. She would finally be strong enough to perform in the final two performances that week. But in the meantime, she was not a happy camper. I told her that Heavenly Father had a reason for allowing her to sprain her ankle, and that she needed to figure out what that purpose was. Carrie made it clear that she did not want to hear that at that moment. But she later admitted I was right.

We had an additional rehearsal the next morning and we opened the Nauvoo Pageant that night, Tuesday, July 11. Before the evening rehearsal, the brother who voiced Carrie's blessing, Brother Remund, came to me with his tears in his eyes and thanked me for asking him to give Carrie's blessing. He told me that earlier that morning, he had asked Heavenly Father if he could be given the opportunity to minister to someone that day. He felt that giving Carrie's blessing was an answer to prayer. I agreed with him as we hugged.

As opening night began, I realized why I had put myself through such suffering. The Spirit was so strong! It was all worth it. All the sweat and sleep deprivation was worth it to feel the Spirit on that stage.

There were two scenes in the Nauvoo Pageant that were particularly meaningful to me. The first was the beginning and ending of a scene called "Evening Dance." At the beginning of the scene, a lone fiddler comes on stage and plays a beautiful waltz while Joseph and Emma dance on stage. Listening to that tune while standing in a field in Nauvoo, on a beautiful, starlit summer night, with a breeze wafting through . . . it is one of the most peaceful moments that I have ever felt in my life. Even before I joined the Church, it was one of my favorite moments in the pageant. Just pure peace for the seconds that tune played.

At the end of the scene, it is made to look like everyone on stage is saying their evening prayers. And we really were! Every district would gather to a specific spot on the stage and say a prayer. A member of the district would be pre-selected to lead their district in prayer while the music is playing softly, and the lights fade. It was such a sweet experience.

The other really meaningful moment was after the temple was built. There is a very powerful scene after the martyrdom of the Prophet where Brigham Young rallies the Saints to complete the temple. Then, the brethren (with the help of the work crew) raise the framework of the temple and the sisters help raise the fabric panels representing the temple exterior. After the temple is "completed," certain members of the family cast were allowed to "enter" the temple. I was one of those selected to go in. Before I walked into the temple, I would always look back at my kids and wave to them. My kids are not members, and it was just my way of showing them that I wished they could join me in the temple someday. This scene was also special to me because of my father.

In 2002, I attended the open house of the Nauvoo temple. Because the Nauvoo temple was so special, I went more than once. During one of those trips, my father, Raymond "Gene" Ready, went with me. He loved woodworking and was greatly impressed with the craftsmanship inside the temple. In 2007, my father was killed in a tragic accident. After I became a member in 2016, I was baptized for him in the St. Louis Missouri Temple. However, I did not receive my endowment until June 27, 2017. When I realized I would be in Nauvoo on my father's birthday (July 11), I determined to perform his endowment in the Nauvoo Temple, because he had been with me in that temple for the open house.

On Tuesday morning, July 11, we held the dress rehearsal for the Nauvoo Pageant. The scene came where we completed the temple. As I walked up the stage to go into the temple, I looked back at my children and waved to them, and then I proceeded to enter the temple. As I looked through the doors of the Nauvoo Temple on the stage, I could see the real Nauvoo temple standing on the hill. It dawned on me that in a few hours, I would be walking through those doors for my father's endowment. It was a powerful moment. That evening during the performance, as I entered the temple on stage, I was reminded of what I had done just a few hours previous. It was a powerful moment each night.

Once the performances started, time really flew. Before we knew it, it was Friday. We had a cast picnic that Friday afternoon. During the picnic, many of the youth got together, played games, and ran around. Carrie could not join them because she was on crutches. While she was sitting there watching her friends have their fun, she noticed a little girl sitting all by herself. Carrie went over to her and began talking to her. She found out that this girl had recently lost a sibling and she was having a hard time. Carrie was able to talk to her and comfort her. Carrie later told me that she realized that if she didn't have a sprained ankle, she would have been hanging with her friends. She would have missed the opportunity to minister to this little girl. God had His reasons. Carrie would find out later that God had another reason for her participation in the pageant. Carrie became close friends with our district Leader, Hannah. Hannah and a member of our family cast, Hunter, became very interested in one another. Carrie was among those who played matchmaker, and now Hannah and Hunter are married!

All too soon, the pageant was over. As the pageant closed, there were tears, goodbyes, and "I love you's" as we scattered back to our homes. Carrie, Caleb, and I spent the night in Nauvoo, attended sacrament meeting that morning, ate dinner in the cafeteria, and decided to visit Carthage Jail on the way home. Several other cast members had the same idea. We said our final goodbyes at Carthage and headed home.

Since Carrie was only able to perform the last two nights of the pageant, I knew I would have to apply at least one more time so she could have a chance to perform. As providence would have it, we were accepted into the 2018 Pageant Family Cast as well.

Preparation for the 2018 Pageant was a lot smoother because I knew what to expect. We made other housing arrangements. They were a little more expensive, but it was worth it not to have to sleep in a woodshed and to have good air conditioning. A few weeks out, I posted a note on a Facebook page for pageant cast members. It was advice, based upon experience, that I wished someone had given me.

For those participating in the Nauvoo/British Pageants for the first time . . .

Hard to believe in less than two months we'll be in Nauvoo preparing for the Nauvoo and British Pageants. Our family is looking forward to seeing old friends and making new ones. For those of you who have never participated in the pageant before, you are in for a very powerful experience. Start praying now for Nauvoo (if you haven't already begun). You will face opposition in this journey! (2 Nephi 2:11) Over the next two months, and even during your time in Nauvoo, you will face opposition—financial difficulties, sickness, injuries, car problems, housing issues, just to name a few possibilities. Don't be surprised when these things happen to you; and do not be afraid, because God will be with you. He will perform miracles for you in ways you cannot imagine.

If you're out of shape (and most of us are) the first week in Nauvoo will be brutal (for us adults—the kids will have the time of their lives). Adjusting to the humidity, 16-hour days, long rehearsals (standing outside on a slanted stage for the most part). At some time during this first week you will probably ask yourselves why are you spending this much money and vacation time on self-inflicted torture. You will never, ever look forward to a Sabbath day more than you will the 2nd Sunday you're there!

Then the performances start. And the Spirit is SO STRONG!!! It's incredible, all the work you put in, all the trials you faced will be more than worth it. And way too soon it will be the last Saturday night, you will say tear-filled goodbyes to all your new friends, your brothers and sisters. And it will be time to go home. And you begin to count the days until it's time to apply for next year.

I write this to you, because I wish someone had given me this heads-up before I participated in the Pageant for the first time. I encourage others who have participated in the pageant to add their experiences below. I know I'd love to read them. Until Nauvoo.

A few weeks ahead of time, the kids started giving me dance lessons again. I was still horrible with the dances. Caleb, Carrie, and I arrived in Nauvoo on Sunday night for orientation. The first week was just as grueling as it had been last year, but I had some good news. I was chosen to hold a banner in one of the dance scenes, so I didn't have to learn that dance! I was so happy.

District meeting was still a favorite time for me. We were in the Sidney district this time with the Turley family—Alex and Chauncey and their children Gideon, Magdalene, and Zacharias. Our district leader this year was Becky Seehootoorah.

Other than the usual sweat and sleep deprivation, the first week of rehearsals were not that remarkable. Although I did find myself using duct tape a lot. About the third night in, I was taking a shower in our cabin (the shower stall was barely big enough to turnaround in), and my daughter had left her razor in one of the soap trays, blade side up. I bumped into it with my elbow and sliced some skin off my arm. There was blood everywhere. I knew there was no way I could keep a bandage on with all the sweating we did, so I put some antibiotic and gauze on it and wrapped it up in duct tape. That way it would be two or three days before it would sweat off completely. A few days later, my glasses fell apart on me during one of the evening rehearsals. Now I can't see worth a darn without my glasses, especially at night, so—more duct tape. Luckily, Carrie was able to help me fix them back at the cabin. But for a while it seemed like duct tape would be my constant companion.

We made it through that first week of rehearsals and enjoyed that blessed Sabbath. The next day, *boom*, another person sprained ankle. Thankfully, it wasn't Carrie this time. But Carrie was able to encourage the person who twisted his ankle. Thankfully, the sprain wasn't as severe, and he was able to make all the performances.

Again, we were in Nauvoo on my Father's birthday. This year I decided I would wait and perform his sealing to his parents on his birthday in the Nauvoo Temple. Again, it made the experience going into the temple on stage all the more powerful.

Another highlight of the 2018 pageant was getting to know one of the assistant directors, Alan Sackett, his lovely wife, Amy, and their young family. We had met the previous year, but this year Alan was really carrying a heavy load. He was playing the role of Heber C. Kimball as well as helping with the directing team and being a father to his young family. Every night I made a point to tell Alan he was doing a great job. He really was! Amy served alongside her husband and performed in the family cast. She was my part-time dance partner. My family loved her.

Though the kids had a fun time, and Carrie was especially enjoying herself since she could participate fully, I was kind of in a funk. Sometimes, being a member of the Church can be very lonely. Once the day-to-day grind of rehearsals were over, the kids would go off and hang out with their friends. Most of the adults in the family cast are married and they would be off doing things with their spouses. Since I was a married man (whose wife was not a member), it would not do well for me to hang out with the single sisters. I would often find myself very lonely. Things also felt quite different this year. I could not put my finger on it, something was missing. I remember having a conversation with a member of the Core Cast, Jake Slater (who has since become a good friend). Jake asked me why I thought the Lord brought me to Nauvoo this year. I didn't have an answer. I didn't know.

In 2017, I didn't want the pageant to end. In 2018, I couldn't wait for the pageant to end. I was hot, tired, and grumpy. We stopped by Carthage on the way home again. During the drive from Nauvoo, Carrie relayed to me an experience she had while we were performing the British Pageant the past Friday Night. Towards the end of the pageant, we sing the following lyric:

Oh, what songs of the heart
We shall sing all the day,
When again we assemble at home,
When we meet ne'er to part
With the blest o'er the way,
There no more from our loved ones to roam!

Tho our rapture and bliss
There's no song can express,
We will shout, we will sing o'er and o'er,
As we greet with a kiss,
And with joy we caress
All our loved ones that passed on before;

As we greet with a kiss,
In our rapture and bliss,
All our loved ones that passed on before.[10]

Carrie said that as she sang these words, she looked out at the back of the crowd and saw her grandfather (my father) standing in the back next to the tent where they have the sound equipment. She said he was watching her and smiling! Carrie had always regretted that her grandfather never had the opportunity to see her perform. But he was there that night. Her experience strengthened my testimony of temple work and gave me a touch of "holy envy." I wish I could have seen him. But I'm glad she did.

After a few good nights of sleep, I pondered Jake's question again. Why did the Lord have me go back to Nauvoo in 2018? Was it just so Carrie could perform? Partially. Finally, it hit me. In 2017, I went to Nauvoo to be ministered to. I was a new member, my experiences in Nauvoo were very powerful to me. But in 2018, I was supposed to go to Nauvoo to be the one doing the ministering! I had blown it big time. Why didn't I see that earlier?! I supposed I was successful in ministering to some. But I certainly missed some important opportunities. That August, we drove back up to Nauvoo for closing night of the pageant. Afterwards, I posted the following on my Facebook page.

A Tale of Two Nauvoos

Though I had seen the pageant just about every year since it opened in 2005, last year was my first year participating. We had our share of trials last year (as everyone does), but I finished my participation in Red Cast 2017 not wanting the Pageant to end. I went home filled with the enthusiasm of the Pageant. We went back up for the final weekend to say goodbye to everyone. But we left before the final performance. I just didn't want to see the Pageant close. The Spirit had been so strong and I wanted to hold on to that feeling as long as I could.

This year, I was relieved when Red Cast 2018 was done performing. Though I didn't want to leave Nauvoo, I was happy to be done with the grind of the Pageant. Before we left, I was

10. "Oh, What Songs of the Heart," *Hymns*, no. 286.

asked by a Core Cast member what I received from being in the Pageant. I didn't have an answer. I went home feeling drained and soon became very depressed. I didn't understand why I felt so differently than the year before.

In time, the Lord led me to realize that last year the Pageant ministered to me. This year it was my turn to minister to the Pageant. I wish I could have figured that out before my time in Red Cast 2018 was over. I would have handled a few situations a little differently. But I hope I succeeded in ministering to some others along the way.

This past weekend we went to see the Pageant close. This time we stayed to the very end and watched them begin to haul away the chairs after the Nauvoo Pageant closed. Though saying goodbye to good friends is always hard, I needed the closure this year. And the joy of having served in Nauvoo has returned.

I don't know if I will ever serve in family cast again, but rest assured, next year, Lord willing, for at least one hot summer night, I will be one among the thousands sitting on that beautiful green cheering on my friends as they make Britvoo come to life once again. I can't wait.

Until next year, Godspeed to all my friends who served in Core Cast, Family Cast and behind the scenes of Nauvoo 2018.

I hope to make it back to Nauvoo and participate in the family cast at least one more time. I'd really love to be able to make up for the opportunities I missed in 2018.

Chapter 10

Check Points

Shortly after my baptism and confirmation, I was ordained to the Aaronic Priesthood by Brother Don Dubree, a good friend and one of the few in my local ward who had never given up on me. Months later he would also ordain me to the Melchizedek Priesthood. I wish we could have recorded the blessing Brother Dubree gave to me at my ordination. I do not remember the words he said, but I do remember the power that I felt in the room during both of my ordinations. Brother Dubree gave me a card that had his Priesthood Line of Authority. It was incredible to see how few names stood between me and Brigham Young and between Brigham Young and Jesus Christ.

Though I didn't feel comfortable giving my daughter a priesthood blessing when she injured her ankle, I've had the opportunity to give a few since then. They have always been very humbling and powerful experiences. As a pastor I prayed for many people, and I often felt God's power working through those prayers. I remember asking an elders quorum instructor to explain to me the difference between a prayer and a blessing. He said that when you pray, you are asking God for a blessing. When you bless someone, you are giving that person the blessing God wants them to have. Or, in other words, when you pray you are asking God to do something. When you give a blessing, you are telling that person what God is going to do for them. To have the authority to speak the words of God to a person is a very humbling and intense experience.

Entering the temple for the first time was a momentous experience. And a bit nerve-racking. For some reason, the person at the recommend desk was not familiar with the type of limited use recommend I had. For a few minutes, I wasn't sure if he would let me in. Luckily, my bishop was there, and he and the temple president were able to sort things out.

When you walk into the temple, it feels like you are walking into another dimension. The pressures of the world just seem to melt away. I remember the joy that I felt as I was able to be baptized for my father and other relatives who had passed on. I don't know if all my relatives have accepted the gospel on the other side, but I am thankful that I had the opportunity to give them the opportunity. Many Christians believe that there is no opportunity to repent after death. Once you die, your eternal destiny is sealed. Latter-day Saints teach that, for most, there will be opportunities to repent and accept the gospel after death. If there is the slightest chance that I can help my ancestors accept the gospel on the other side of the veil, I want to take it.

I went through the endowment ceremony for the first time on June 27, 2016, the 172nd anniversary of the martyrdom of the Prophet Joseph Smith. Brothers Lynn Ennis and Don Dubree went with me for my first time. I was nervous and excited. So nervous in fact, that I walked right past one of my former missionaries, Kirk Philips. Lynn had told Kirk that I was going to the temple for the first time. Kirk flew in from Las Vegas that morning to be able to attend the temple with me. I didn't recognize him at first, but it meant a lot having him there with me.

Having studied the Church for so long, I had an idea of what to expect when I went through the ceremony. But what I didn't anticipate was the peace that you feel when you enter the celestial room. I've returned to the temple several times to participate in these ceremonies for my ancestors. But I must confess, I often return for selfish reasons—to enjoy the peace I feel when I'm there.

My callings in the Church so far include chorister, choir director, first counselor in the Sunday School presidency, first and second counselor in the elders quorum presidency, and ward temple and family history coordinator. My current calling is co-teaching one of the youth Sunday School classes with my oldest son. Each calling has had it rewards and challenges. I believe my greatest success so far came during my service as chorister when I was able to increase the tempo of the congregational hymns by five beats per minute!

Of all the ordinances I've experienced thus far, the most powerful for me was the patriarchal blessing. I had been a member for about eight months when I received my blessing. I was instructed to fast and pray to prepare myself for this experience. I did and I was not disappointed. As the patriarch laid his hands upon my head, I felt as if I was enveloped in a warm blanket. It was like that feeling you get when you wake up on a cold winter morning, snuggled under a pile of blankets, drifting in and out of sleepiness. A feeling of perfect peace and contentment. I didn't want it to end. I didn't want to "wake up."

Listening to the words of the patriarch raised many questions in my mind as he spoke about the pre-mortal realm and the things I would see the Lord do, and the things he would do through me in this life, if I was faithful. Afterwards, we discussed the impressions I felt and the questions I had. He clarified a few things for me and told me that my best bet was to go straight to the Lord and ask Him. One of the greatest blessings he gave me was the blessing that I would be sealed in the temple if I am faithful. A few well-meaning members have asked me if I was worried about missing out on the blessing of a temple marriage since my wife is not a member of the Church. Because of my patriarchal blessing, I am not worried. The Lord told me I would be sealed in the temple as long as I'm faithful.

Some Latter-day Saints may see these experiences and ordinances as a list of things that they need to accomplish in order to enter the celestial kingdom. It is easy to see the principles of the gospel—faith, repentance, baptism, gift of the Holy Ghost, endowments, temple marriage, enduring to the end—as a heavenly checklist. But I view them differently. I do not see these steps as boxes on a checklist. I see them as checkpoints on a map.

When I was a pastor, missionaries would often ask me what would happen if I was wrong about the Church. Would I not regret missing out on the opportunity to go to the celestial kingdom? I told them I was not worried about that. When I was fourteen years old, I committed my life to Jesus Christ. I was following and trusting Him. If Jesus wanted me to get to the celestial kingdom, He would get me there. I didn't get baptized and confirmed because I was trying to earn anything or trying to tick boxes on a list. I was baptized and confirmed because that is what I believe Jesus wanted me to do. When I had the opportunity to serve in callings or attend the temple, I did not do those things because I was trying to gain God's favor. I did those things because I believed He wanted me to do them. I did them because I loved Him, and I wanted to serve Him.

The Spirit I felt as I experienced these things was confirmation to me that I was on the right path. When I was ordained to the priesthood. When I received my temple recommend. These were the checkpoints that confirmed to me that I was still on the right path.

I remember one time when I was hiking with my children on a trail at a nearby state park. The trail was marked by yellow diamonds painted on trees and signposts every so often. I don't remember what happened, but the kids and I became distracted and got off the trail somehow. It wasn't intentional, and I don't think we strayed very far, but it was far enough for me to become disoriented. I cannot tell you the relief I felt when I finally found a tree with a yellow diamond painted on to it. I was back on the right trail! To me, these saving ordinances are like those yellow diamond trail markers, wonderful reminders that I was on the right path.

Concluding Thoughts

OVER THE PAST FEW YEARS, MANY PERSONS OF OTHER FAITHS HAVE asked me, "Why in the world did you want to become a Mormon?" To be honest, I don't know all the reasons. I feel like these people—the Latter-day Saints—are my people. These are the people to whom and among whom God has called me to minister, and I feel assured that God has called me to join them.

Among all the teachings of the restored Church, I really appreciate our belief in temple work, that in some way we can help those who have passed on and now reside on the other side of the veil. Though this idea of being linked to persons who have died is foreign to Protestants, it is not foreign to the theology of the Roman Catholic and Orthodox Christian traditions. I am very comforted by the belief that families can be together forever.

I can testify of the reality of personal revelation—the belief that God will speak to you if you will just ask (this is a personal belief I had as a Baptist as well). I also appreciate that in The Church of Jesus Christ of Latter-day Saints, Jesus and American history intersect in a unique and powerful way. That Jesus walked on this continent; and that America wasn't merely a product of historical forces but is indeed a chosen land of God. I believe these things are true.

I also still hold to many of the truths that I learned as a Southern Baptist. I still believe in the exclusivity of the gospel of Jesus Christ. No man comes to the Father but through Jesus. I still believe in justification by grace alone, through faith alone. I will discuss these and other beliefs in the appendix. I still love Southern Baptists and the theological education I received at Baptist institutions—especially The Southern Baptist Theological Seminary. I really wish our two groups could get along a little better. We certainly hold many social, moral, and family values in common. As Western culture becomes more and more anti-Christian, it would be in our best interest to link arms and work together where we can and engage in civil discussions about our differences.

For those of you who are not yet members of The Church of Jesus Christ of Latter-day Saints, I understand the barriers that you may be facing—questions about the Church, questions about theology, objections from family. Seek the Lord and He will give you the answers you need. I believe the Lord is getting ready to do a mighty work through this Church. I would love for you to be a part of it. I can now testify to you of the truthfulness of the words of President Gordon B. Hinckley, "Bring with you all that you have of good and truth which you have received from whatever source, and come and let us see if we may add to it." Come on in. The water's fine.

I hope my story will be an encouragement to any readers experiencing trials. One of our most beautiful and fundamental beliefs is that God is still speaking. He will answer the prayer of anyone who asks with a sincere heart. If you are looking for answers, pray to Heavenly Father expecting an answer and He will answer! It may not be the answer you want, but He will answer.

He answers in different ways. He will answer you through the scriptures. As you read the scriptures, verses may pop out at you, providing needed answers. He will answer you through other people. My decision to follow Christ came in response to an invitation from another person. At different times in my life, various people would come up to me and tell me that they felt that God was going to call me to be a pastor. I didn't believe them. I didn't want to believe them. But they were right, and God used them to prepare me for that calling. God will speak to you also, through the power of His Holy Spirit. That still, small voice (1 Kings 19:12) will whisper to you in your mind or in your heart. The impression may come as a thought that suddenly floats into your mind. It will be familiar to you, but you will recognize that it did not come from within you, but from the Spirit. Our Father in Heaven may also answer you in the form of dreams or visions. They are not common but be mindful and aware of your dreams as you seek answers. As you pray and seek, you must learn to trust in the Lord's timing. That can be the hardest thing to do. Look how long it took the Lord to prepare the way for me to join the Church. The wait was excruciating at times. But God's timing was perfect.

Finally, I would like to bear my testimony that I know Jesus is the Christ, the Son of God. He loves you. He died for you. I know that the scripture is true that if you place your faith and trust in Him, you will never perish but have everlasting life (John 3:16). Just pray to your Heavenly Father. Tell Him you are committing your life to Jesus Christ. Your life will never be the same! I testify to you of the truthfulness of the Restoration, the truthfulness of the Book of Mormon, and the power of God that is manifest in The Church of Jesus Christ of Jesus Christ of Latter-day Saints.

Appendix

Theological Thinking

"Bring with you all that you have of good and truth which you have received from whatever source, and come and let us see if we may add to it."

—President Gordon B. Hinckley

As I mentioned earlier, I really needed to know if what President Hinckley said was true. I held some doctrinal convictions that were very important to me. I did not want to sacrifice these convictions to join the Church. Could I really bring what I have into the Church and be a member in good standing? I also had to make peace with the Prophet Joseph Smith. For many years, I was convinced he was a fraud. How could I accept him as a prophet? The sections in this appendix provide a summary of my beliefs on these important issues. Though they don't really go into the process of how I got to this point, they are a reflection of where I am in this still ongoing process. These statements do not represent official doctrine, either from The Church of Jesus Christ of Latter-day Saints or the Southern Baptists. They are simply my beliefs. I'm including them here because they are integral to my story. I also hope that they might be helpful to the reader, especially those seeking to understand the differences between The Church of Jesus Christ of Latter-day Saints and other Christian groups. I hope that they might help these faiths to find a path to work together in these trying times, and also helpful to those who might be thinking about joining the church, at least to show them how one Southern Baptist did it.

Though I don't always quote him directly, Dr. Shon Hopkin's dialogue with me was an invaluable part of this process. We have hundreds of pages of e-mails where we discussed and debated our theological differences. I would not be writing this book without Shon's willingness to help me work through my questions (and of course, his willingness to baptize me!) Thank you, Shon. You are a much-loved brother and friend.

Rethinking Joseph Smith Jr.

For years I have been studying the life of this unique American religious leader. For most of those years I viewed him as a fraud. I often viewed him as the "Moriarty" to my "Holmes" (A delusion of grandeur to be sure, but it was a fun delusion). Over time, my perspective on Joseph radically changed. I now believe that he was a prophet called by God to establish The Church of Jesus Christ of Latter-day Saints. Here are three things that helped me change my mind: (1) Joseph's capacity for forgiveness; (2) his death; and (3) the likelihood of "a lying spirit."

Joseph's Capacity for Forgiveness

Christianity is the only religion that commands its followers to forgive (Matthew 18:21–22). Other religions may hold forgiveness as a virtue, but only Christians are commanded to forgive. Indeed, we are told that if we do not forgive, our sins will not be forgiven (Matthew 18:35). I would argue that forgiveness is one of the hardest things a Christian is commanded to do. It's something we simply cannot do without Christ's help. It is clear that Joseph was more than willing to forgive people who asked for it. Consider the story of W.W. Phelps.

W.W. Phelps was a close associate of Joseph Smith Jr. During the intense persecutions of the Church in Missouri, Phelps had a falling out with Joseph and was excommunicated from the Church. Phelps signed an affidavit that accused Joseph of many wrongdoings. This affidavit, in part, led to Joseph's incarceration in the Liberty Jail for nearly five months. Conditions were horrible in that jail. Joseph, and the other church leaders incarcerated with him, barely survived. After Joseph and the other leaders were released, they made their way to Illinois and established the community of Nauvoo, Illinois.

In June 1840, Phelps wrote a letter to Joseph asking for forgiveness and re-baptism into the Church. Joseph responded with the following:

> *Dear Brother Phelps*
>
> *I must say that it is with no ordinary feelings I endeavour to write a few lines to you in answer to [your letter], at the same time I am rejoiced at the privilege granted me. You may in some measure realise what my feelings, as well as Elder Rigdon's & Bro Hyrum's were when we read your letter, truly our hearts were melted into tenderness and compassion when we ascertained your resolves &c. . . .*
>
> *It is true, that we have suffered much in consequence of your behavior—the cup of gall already full enough for mortals to drink, was indeed filled to overflowing when you turned against us: . . .*
>
> *However the cup has been drunk, the will of our heavenly Father has been done, and we are yet alive for which we thank the Lord. And having been delivered from the hands of wicked men by the mercy of our God, we say it is your privilidge to be delivered from the power of the Adversary . . .*
>
> *Believing your confession to be real and your repentance genuine, I shall be happy once again to give you the right hand of fellowship and rejoice over the returning prodigal. . . .*
>
> *"Come on dear Brother since the war is past, For friends at first are friends again at last."*
>
> *Yours as Ever*
> *Joseph Smith Jr.*[11]

I don't know if I could have forgiven someone, especially a close friend, whose false testimony resulted in my being thrown into jail.

11. Joseph Smith Jr., "Letter to William W. Phelps, 22 July 1840," p. 158, The Joseph Smith Papers, accessed April 23, 2020, https://www.josephsmithpapers.org/paper-summary/letter-to-william-w-phelps-22-july-1840/2.

I don't think there is any way, apart from Christ, that I could have extended forgiveness. I don't think there was any way Joseph could have done it, apart from Christ. Joseph would also forgive other men who had turned against him at various times, including Orson Hyde, Orson Pratt, and Parley Pratt. Joseph's capacity for forgiveness is a strong testimony to his divine calling.

Joseph's Death

History is filled with religious charlatans—men and women—deceivers, who claimed to have "the truth." Their movements make a big splash and then they disappear. A few create organizations that survive their deaths—Ellen G. White (Seventh-day Adventists), Charles Taze Russell (Jehovah's Witnesses), and Mary Baker Eddy (Christian Science) come to mind. Most of these "visionaries" lived relatively long lives and died in relative prosperity. A few have gone out in a "blaze of glory" so to speak, such as Jim Jones, David Koresh, and Marshall Applewhite.[12] There are other false teachers today who preach the so-called "prosperity gospel"—a "name it and claim it" message teaching that God wants all of His children to be financially prosperous—and live in the lap of luxury themselves.

---

12. Jim Jones (1931–1978), an American religious leader, led his followers to the jungles of Guyana, South America, where they established an "agricultural" commune. When rumors of human rights abuses reached the United States, a Congressional delegation was sent to investigate. As the delegation prepared to depart, Jones's militia attacked, killing several members of the delegation. That evening, Jones ordered his 909 followers to drink flavor-aid laced with cyanide. Jones died from a self-inflicted gunshot wound.

David Koresh (aka Vernon Howell, 1959–1993) was the leader of the Branch Davidians, an offshoot from the Seventh Day Adventists. In 1993, Federal ATF agents raided Koresh's headquarters and a gunfight ensued killing four ATF agents. A siege resulted. Koresh refused to surrender or allow any of his followers to leave. On April 19, 1993 government agents began pumping tear gas into the compound. A fire then broke out killing 79 people. It was later discovered that Koresh had been killed by a gunshot wound to the head.

Marshall Applewhite (1931–1997) founded the religious group "Heaven's Gate." In March 1997, Applewhite and his thirty-eight followers committed suicide believing that in so doing they could rendezvous with an alien spaceship following the Hale-Bopp Comet. The spaceship would take them on to heaven.

Throughout history, these leaders have milked their people for their money and, at times, have demanded their lives. Jones and Applewhite ordered the death of their people and killed themselves. Koresh ordered his people to resist federal agents and died with them in the ensuing inferno (some, including Koresh, died by suicide). But in contrast to these men, Joseph Smith's story is very different. How is Joseph different? He died *for* his people.

Tensions were high in Hancock County Illinois in 1844. Throughout their history (and for various reasons), conflict swirled around the Latter-day Saints and their leaders. The citizens of Illinois, which had initially provided a refuge for the Latter-day Saints, were rapidly becoming hostile to them. In June of 1844, Joseph Smith, Mayor of Nauvoo, and the city council ordered the destruction of a newspaper (the Nauvoo Expositor) critical of Smith and his leadership. The owners of the press went to the county seat, Carthage, IL, and swore out warrants for the arrest of Smith and the other town leaders. But this was not enough for many of the old citizens of Hancock county who were enraged. Years of perceived favoritism by politicians, Joseph Smith's ability to circumvent county and state laws through the courts of Nauvoo, as well as rumors of polygamy and sexual immorality served as dry tinder for the spark that was the destruction of the Expositor press.[13]

13. The Nauvoo Expositor was published by Church dissidents who broke with Joseph Smith over teachings related to plural marriage and exaltation. Many critics argue that Joseph had the press destroyed because he did not want these teachings exposed. Though Joseph was secretly teaching plural marriage to a few select church leaders at that time, he was publicly teaching the doctrine of exaltation (ex. The King Follett Discourse). It wasn't just the exposure of the teachings which was troubling, it was the way the paper was portraying Joseph and his teachings. One article called Joseph a "blood thirsty and murderous . . . demon . . . in human shape" and "a syncophant (sic), whose attempt for power find no parallel in history . . . one of the blackest and basest scoundrels that has appeared upon the stage of human existence since the days of Nero, and Caligula" (Francis M. Higbee, "Citizens of Hancock County," Nauvoo Expositor [7 June 1844]). This inflammatory rhetoric led to genuine fears that the Expositor would embolden the enemies of the Church and spark mob violence like the Saints had endured in Missouri. Joseph wasn't the only one concerned. The Nauvoo City Council (which included some non-Church members) voted unanimously to declare the Nauvoo Expositor a public nuisance and have it removed from the city.

Consider the words of Thomas Sharp, the editor of a neighboring community's newspaper, The Warsaw Signal, just before and after the Expositor incident.

> *We have seen and heard enough to convince us that Joe Smith is not safe out of Nauvoo, and we would not be surprised to hear of his death by violent means in a short time. He has deadly enemies — men whose wrongs have maddened them.*
>
> *. . . The feeling of this country is now lashed to its utmost pitch, and will break forth in fury upon the slightest provocation . . .*[14]

> *"We have only to state, that this is sufficient! War and extermination is inevitable! Citizens ARISE, ONE and ALL!!! — Can you stand by and suffer such INFERNAL DEVILS!! to ROB men of their property and RIGHTS, without avenging them. We have no time for comment, every man will make his own. LET IT BE MADE WITH POWDER AND BALL!!!"*[15]

Joseph was worried for his own life and the lives of his people. He was being warned that mobs were amassing and if Smith and his city councilors did not surrender, the city would be attacked. Now, Smith had at his call the Nauvoo Legion, a militia with over 2,000 men. He could have easily called up the Legion, fortified Nauvoo, and engaged in a bloody civil war with the neighboring militias. But he did not do that. It became obvious to Smith that he was the primary target of the legal action and the antagonism of the neighboring communities. He felt that if he were to leave town, things would calm down and the residents of Nauvoo would be safe. So, he left for the West. He didn't get very far when a delegation of leaders from Nauvoo sought him out. Some of his followers thought he was deserting them. Others accused him of cowardice. Smith is reported to have said, "If my life is of no value to my friends, it is of no value to me." Smith did return, assisted in the disarming of the Nauvoo legion, surrendered to officials in Carthage, and was murdered at the hands of an angry mob in Carthage, Illinois on June 27, 1844. Smith reportedly made another

---

14. Sharp, Thomas. Editorial. Warsaw Signal. May 29, 1844.
15. ________ "Unparalleled Outrage at Nauvoo." Warsaw Signal. June 12, 1844.

comment as he was preparing to leave for Carthage, "I am going like a lamb to the slaughter, but I am as calm as a summer's morning. I have a conscience void of offense toward God and toward all men." Some argue that Joseph never said these things. They argue that Joseph was confident he would again escape from the law. But given the warnings of Thomas Sharp and the Warsaw Signal, he had to know that if the mobs were to get ahold of him, he would be lynched. And that is what happened. Yes, Joseph attempted to defend himself and the other men in the upper room of Carthage Jail. But, when faced with impending doom, he didn't order his followers to kill themselves or to fortify the city and prepare for battle. He did what he thought he needed to do to save his people, not just his own life. That's pretty odd behavior for a huckster, don't you think? As a matter of fact, I can't think of any other known "fraud" in the history of Christendom who sacrificed himself for his people. "Greater love hath no man than this, that a man lay down his life for his friends" (John 15:13).

A Lying Spirit

The Prophet Joseph Smith was the subject of much discussion in my dialogue with Shon. I remember on one occasion I asked Shon about all the rumors and innuendo that swirled around Joseph. Shon agreed that Joseph was human and probably made his share of mistakes. But he also believed that Joseph was the victim of "a lying spirit" and that many of those rumors were invented to discredit Joseph.

I must admit, I openly scoffed at such a notion. I thought Shon was letting his religious bias get in the way of his critical thinking. I felt that way until I had my own experience with "a lying spirit."

Six months after I was baptized, a close relative died. I found out about it on Facebook. I was stunned no one bothered to call me and tell me. I later found out that my relative's immediate family had heard that I had gotten divorced and that my oldest son and I had moved to Utah!

A few months later, I ran into some old friends at a restaurant. They told me that they had heard that I had left the pastorate, divorced my wife, gotten remarried, and had two kids with my new wife!

As of this writing, I'm still married to Jennifer, and we have lived in the same home for nineteen years. I also now believe in "lying spirits." I was the pastor of a small church. I live in a community of less than six hundred people. If these kinds of stories can be made up about me, imagine what rumors can swirl around the leader of a worldwide church, living in a community that rivaled the size of Chicago! I'm not saying Joseph was infallible. He was human and therefore sinned and made mistakes the same way we all do. But I certainly now understand what Shon meant about a "lying spirit."

Reconciling Friends: The Role of Grace and Works in Salvation

A young woman asked the great Baptist preacher Charles Spurgeon if it was possible to reconcile God's sovereignty and man's responsibility. "Young woman," said he. "You don't reconcile friends." Countless discussions and numerous debates have been held between Baptists and Latter-day Saints on the role of grace and works in salvation. Baptists proclaim, "For by grace are ye saved through faith; and that not of yourselves: it is the gift of God: Not of works, lest any man should boast" (Ephesians 2:8–9). To which Latter-day Saints respond with "faith without works is dead also" (James 2:26).

To complicate matters, Baptists define "grace" as God's "unmerited favor." Whereas Latter-day Saints tend to define "grace" as "God's enabling power." So, which is it? Is there any middle ground? I think so. Here's how. Part of the problem lies in the fact that we tend to forget that salvation is a process. Paul wrote,

We are saved. (Ephesians 2:8)

We are being saved. "For the preaching of the cross is to them that perish foolishness; but unto us which are [being] saved it is the power of God." (1 Corinthians 1:18)

We will be saved. "Much more then, being now justified by his blood, we shall be saved from wrath through him. For if, when we were enemies, we were reconciled to God by the death of his Son, much more, being reconciled, we shall be saved by his life." (Romans. 5:9–10)

When we talk about salvation, we tend to focus on one aspect of salvation rather than the whole process. It's like the parable of the blind men touching different parts of the elephant's body. They do their best to describe what they feel, but they are only focusing on one part of the "animal." Southern Baptists emphasize what happens when a person trusts Christ as their Savior, and they are "saved." Latter-day Saints tend to focus on salvation as something that will happen after death when we receive our eternal reward. We need to remember that salvation is a process.

The process of salvation includes Justification, Sanctification, and Glorification. Consider the following definitions, with which I grew up.

> ***Justification*** *is God's gracious and full acquittal upon principles of His righteousness of all sinners who repent and believe in Christ. Justification brings the believer unto a relationship of peace and favor with God.*
>
> ***Sanctification*** *is the experience . . . by which the believer . . . is enabled to progress toward moral and spiritual maturity through the presence and power of the Holy Spirit dwelling in him.*
>
> ***Glorification*** *is the culmination of salvation and is the final blessed and abiding state of the redeemed.16 [Exaltation would be the Latter-day Saint equivalent of Glorification.]*

Though these are "Baptist" definitions, I've run them by a few Latter-day Saint religious scholars, and they didn't find much disagreement with them.

Justification

When you hear an "Evangelical" talk about being "saved" they are talking about justification. And they see no room for our works in the work of justification. Justification is completely the work of the

16. "IV. Salvation," *Southern Baptist Convention: The Baptist Faith and Message*, 2000, www.sbc.net/bfm2000/bfm2000.asp.

Holy Spirit. When a person repents of their sins and commits their life to Jesus Christ, their sins are whisked through time and imputed to Christ through the Atonement. The righteousness of Christ is then imputed onto the person committing their life. That person is declared "not guilty" by God. At this moment, the person is justified, or "saved" (in Baptist terms).

Here are a few scriptures from the New Testament related to justification:

> *"For by grace [God's unmerited favor] are ye saved through faith; and that not of yourselves: it is the gift of God: Not of works, lest any man should boast." (Ephesians 2:8–9)*

> *"That if thou shalt confess with thy mouth the Lord Jesus, and shalt believe in thine heart that God hath raised him from the dead, thou shalt be saved. For with the heart man believeth unto righteousness; and with the mouth confession is made unto salvation." (Romans 10:9–10)*

> *For all have sinned, and come short of the glory of God; Being justified freely by his grace through the redemption that is in Christ Jesus: Whom God hath set forth to be a propitiation through faith in his blood, to declare his righteousness for the remission of sins that are past, through the forbearance of God;" (Romans 3:23–25)*

> *"For what saith the scripture? Abraham believed God, and it was counted unto him for righteousness. Now to him that worketh is the reward not reckoned of grace, but of debt. But to him that worketh not, but believeth on him that justifieth the ungodly, his faith is counted for righteousness." (Romans 4:3–5)*

> *"He staggered not at the promise of God through unbelief; but was strong in faith, giving glory to God; And being fully persuaded that, what he had promised, he was able also to perform. And therefore it was imputed to him for righteousness. Now it was not written for his sake alone, that it was imputed to him; But for us also, to whom it shall be imputed, if we believe on him that*

raised up Jesus our Lord from the dead; Who was delivered for our offences, and was raised again for our justification." (Romans 4:20–25)

Our justification is completely based on faith and grace (God's unmerited favor). But what about repentance? The act of faith? The act of commitment to Christ? Aren't these works? Let's say for the sake of argument that they are a type of human work. Those "works" are done only in response to something that God is already doing in the person's life. They repent because the Holy Spirit has convicted them. They commit in response to God's invitation. They exercise the faith that God gave to them (Matthew 13:11; 1 Corinthians 12:9). So, even if you believe that faith and repentance are acts of human effort, they are still only possible in response to what God has already done in a person's life. But what about all those verses of scripture that seem to indicate that works do indeed play a role in our salvation? Let us move on to Sanctification and Glorification.

Sanctification

Sanctification is the process by which we become pure, holy, and more Christ-like through God's grace (Doctrine and Covenants 20:31)—through the sanctifying presence and power of the Holy Spirit dwelling in us. Growth in grace should continue throughout the regenerated person's life.

Baptists certainly believe that our works play a role in our sanctification, and though they define "grace" as "God's Unmerited Favor" in justification, they can certainly affirm the restored gospel's emphasis of grace as "God's Enabling Power" in our sanctification. Let's go back to Ephesians 2:8–9 and include verse 10:

"For by grace are ye saved through faith; and that not of yourselves: it is the gift of God: 9 Not of works, lest any man should boast. For we are his workmanship, created in Christ Jesus unto good works, which God hath before ordained that we should walk in them." (Ephesians 2:8–10)

We are "saved" (justified) for the purpose of good works.

> *"Wherefore, my beloved, as ye have always obeyed, not as in my presence only, but now much more in my absence, work out your own salvation with fear and trembling." (Philippians 2:12)*

> *"Pure religion and undefiled before God and the Father is this, To visit the fatherless and widows in their affliction, and to keep himself unspotted from the world." (James 1:27)*

In the Parable of the Talents (Matthew 25:14–30) and the Barren Fig Tree (Luke 13:6–9), Jesus certainly indicates that God expects us to bear fruit and use the talents that God has given us for Him and His glory. And Jesus makes it very clear in the parable of the Vine and Branches (John 15:5) that we *cannot* do any good works *without* Him. 1 Corinthians 12:27 tells us we are the body of Christ.

As we do the works of Christ through God's enabling power, we become more like Christ. We become sanctified. And one day we will be rewarded for those works in our glorification.

Glorification

Glorification is the culmination of salvation and is the final blessed and abiding state of the redeemed. All Christians agree that we will be rewarded for our works. Paul makes this very clear in 1 Corinthians 3:11–15:

> *For other foundation can no man lay than that is laid, which is Jesus Christ. Now if any man build upon this foundation gold, silver, precious stones, wood, hay, stubble; Every man's work shall be made manifest: for the day shall declare it, because it shall be revealed by fire; and the fire shall try every man's work of what sort it is. If any man's work abide which he hath built thereupon, he shall receive a reward. If any man's work shall be burned, he shall suffer loss: but he himself shall be saved; yet so as by fire.*

The role our works play in glorification is clearly illustrated by the Savior in the Parable of the Sheep and Goats (Matthew 25:31–46). For in the end, a person's place in the kingdom depended on what they did or did not do.

Not only are we rewarded for our works, but there also seem to be levels of punishment for evil works. Jesus said,

> *But I say unto you, that it shall be more tolerable in that day for Sodom, than for that city. Woe unto thee, Chorazin! woe unto thee, Bethsaida! for if the mighty works had been done in Tyre and Sidon, which have been done in you, they had a great while ago repented, sitting in sackcloth and ashes. But it shall be more tolerable for Tyre and Sidon at the judgment, than for you. (Luke 10:12–14)*

To summarize, Baptists believe that we are justified only by God's grace (Unmerited Favor). God's grace (enabling power) enables us to serve Him and become more like Him. Our works play an essential role in our sanctification and glorification and those works would not be possible without God's grace (His divine assistance, His gifts, and His enabling power). Once we blind men and women get a glimpse at the whole elephant of salvation, we see that we have much more in common than we have disagreement when it comes to the roles of grace and works in our salvation.

The Trinity

I would assert that the most significant difference between the doctrine of The Church of Jesus Christ of Latter-day Saints and traditional Christianity is the concept of the Godhead. Millions of pages have been written on the subject of God and the Trinity. I'm only going to write a few. I'm not trying to argue that anyone should accept this view, but there is such a wide divide between Latter-day Saints and other Christian groups on this issue. I wanted to take a crack at bridging it, or to at least show people how I bridged it. Very few people (Latter-day Saint or other Christians) really understand the historic Christian doctrine of the Trinity. So, I'm going to start with a brief explanation of how the doctrine of the Trinity came to be and provide an illustration that I used when I was pastoring.

Latter-day Saints rightly argue that the word "Trinity" is not found in the New Testament. The word was actually coined by Tertullian, an early church leader around AD 200. Christians coming out of the strict monotheism of Judaism struggled to reconcile the fact that the scriptures attest that the Father is God (1 Corinthians 8:6), Jesus is God (John 1:1), and the Holy Spirit is God (2 Corinthians 3:3) with the Hebrew view that there is only one God. They wanted to make sure that Christians understood that Jesus Christ and the Holy Ghost are fully divine, and not merely a human representative or divine emanation.

Latter-day Saints also rightly argue that doctrine of the Trinity is rooted in Greek philosophy. But in fairness, that is to be expected. The pedagogy of early Western civilization was rooted in Greek philosophy. For the first 1,000 years after Christ, if you wished to express yourself academically, scientifically, or even theologically you would have done so within a Greek philosophical framework (in much the same way that academics and scientists today are expected to express themselves within a secular/evolutionary framework). That was just the milieu in which the early Church existed. It was not an overt attempt to corrupt or change Christian theology.

During this time, several church councils were held, and different creeds were developed to try and explain important Christian beliefs and refute false teachings. The most famous and foundational Trinitarian Creed is the Athanasian Creed. It describes the Trinity in part.

> *. . . we worship one God in Trinity, and Trinity in Unity;*
>
> *Neither confounding the Persons: nor dividing the Substance.*
>
> *For there is one Person of the Father: another of the Son: and another of the Holy Ghost.*
>
> *But the Godhead of the Father, of the Son, and of the Holy Ghost, is all one: the Glory equal, the Majesty coeternal.*
>
> *Such as the Father is: such is the Son: and such is the Holy Ghost . . .*
>
> *So likewise the Father is Almighty: the Son Almighty: and the Holy Ghost Almighty.*

And yet they are not Three Almighties: but one Almighty.

So the Father is God: the Son is God: and the Holy Ghost is God.

And yet they are not three Gods: but One God.

So likewise the Father is Lord: the Son Lord: and the Holy Ghost Lord.

And yet not three Lords: but One Lord. . . .

So there is one Father, not three Fathers: one Son, not three Sons: One Holy Ghost, not three Holy Ghosts.

And in this Trinity none is afore, or after another: none is greater, or less than another.

But the whole three Persons are coeternal, and coequal.[17]

So this means the Father is God, The Son is God, and The Holy Spirit is God, and they are one God. But the Father is *not* the Son (and vice versa). The Son is *not* the Holy Spirit (and vice versa). The Father is *not* the Holy Spirit (and vice versa). But they are all one God. Clear as mud, right?

I will try and break this down a little more. But before I do that, I want to clarify a common misconception that many have about the Trinity. The historic understanding of the Trinity *does not teach* that God the Father and Jesus are the same person. They are different persons! Again—The Father, Son, and Holy Spirit are three distinct, different, thinking, intelligent beings. They play different roles in the work of creation and salvation, and in some regards have different characteristics. Let me say this one more time: the historic understanding of the Trinity is that Father, Son, and Holy Spirit are three different persons! How do we define persons? It's hard to find a theological definition of "person" that is universal and easy to comprehend. So, until I do, I will use this definition: A person is a thinking, intelligent being who is complete in him/herself, but exists in relationship to

17. Philip Schaff, "IV. Symbolum Quicunque. The Athanasian Creed," *Creeds of Christendom. Vol II.* Retrieved September 21, 2020, from https://www.ccel.org/ccel/schaff/creeds2.iv.i.iv.html.

others. Let me give an illustration. You are a complete, thinking, intelligent being. You are independent. Yet, your relationships have heavily influenced you as a person. You wouldn't be you without the relationships you have had, without the influence (for good or bad) of parents, teachers, coaches, friends, and church leaders. You are an intelligent, thinking being. But you exist in relationship to others.

It's interesting that Latter-day Saints often refer to Jesus's baptism as a refutation of the Trinity. Ironically, Trinitarians point to these verses as proof of the Trinity! They readily affirm that the Father, Son, and Holy Spirit are one God yet three distinct persons. They play different roles in our salvation. They can manifest themselves in different ways, in different places simultaneously but also distinctly.

So where does the "oneness" come from? How can they be one "being" if there are three distinct persons? One illustration I frequently use to describe the Trinity is to look at the oceans of our planet. Let's think about the Atlantic, Pacific, and Indian Oceans. They are three different oceans. The Atlantic is not the Pacific, etc. They have different characteristics, different ecosystems, different locations. But you can't tell where one stops and the other starts. They are distinct and definable but at the same time connected.

Let's look at ourselves. Are we merely "physical beings"? Do we not also have a spirit/soul? There is a metaphysical aspect to our being. When a man and a woman are married, scripture declares that they become one flesh (Genesis 2:24). The physical expression of that is found in sexuality, but is there not also a knitting of the soul/spirit as well? If there is not a knitting of spirits, how could we enjoy our communion as husband and wife in the interim period between death and resurrection? Paul writes, "For this cause shall a man leave his father and mother, and shall be joined unto his wife, and they two shall be one flesh. This is a great mystery" (Ephesians 5:31–32).

Let's take that a step further. Historic Christianity teaches that one member of the Godhead (Jesus) has a physical body. Latter-day Saint Christianity teaches that two members of the Godhead (Jesus and Father) have physical bodies. But are He/They merely physical or do They not also have souls/spirits? No, they have/are spirits as well. If a man and woman can have their spirits knitted together in a small way by God in a marriage ceremony, is it not possible that the spirits of the Father, Son, and Holy Spirit are knitted together eternally? Think about it. Latter-day Saints believe that we are all sons and daughters of Heavenly Father, but we also recognize that there is a unique relationship between the Father and Jesus. Jesus was the only begotten of the Father. We also recognize that the Spirit has a special relationship with the Father and the Son in that He is the only member of the Godhead without a physical body. Then can it not be possible that the Father, Son, and Holy Spirit, though separate and unique persons, have a deep, eternal, ontological, and metaphysical relationship/connection/oneness that we can only begin to comprehend? The belief in that oneness is the essence of the Trinity—three different persons united in an eternal, ontological, and metaphysical oneness.

Baptist Polity

In this section I would like to discuss a few differences between the organization of a Baptist church and a Latter-day Saint ward. I hope this discussion will be helpful to those readers who want to know more about how other Christian churches function. If you aren't interested, feel free to skip over this section.

LOCAL CHURCH LEADERS

In a Southern Baptist church, the pastor is the leader of the local church. There is no denominational hierarchy that has authority over the local church pastor. Only God and local church membership have authority over the pastor. Along with the pastor, other leaders of the church include: trustees, deacons, Women's Ministry Director (sometimes called WMU or Women's Missionary Union leader in Baptist circles), a treasurer, Sunday School director/teachers, children's ministry leaders, and a host of other volunteer leaders and committees.

A trustee is a church member who has been elected to represent the church in temporal matters and function as a legal representative of the church in accordance with the church's articles of incorporation as a non-profit corporation. If the church enters into a contract with someone, for example, mowing the lawn or servicing office equipment, the trustees sign the contract. The trustees also ensure the maintenance and upkeep of church facilities.

A deacon must be an adult male who met the qualifications of 1 Timothy 3:8–13.

> *Likewise must the deacons be grave, not doubletongued, not given to much wine, not greedy of filthy lucre;*
>
> *Holding the mystery of the faith in a pure conscience.*
>
> *And let these also first be proved; then let them use the office of a deacon, being found blameless.*
>
> *Even so must their wives be grave, not slanderers, sober, faithful in all things.*
>
> *Let the deacons be the husbands of one wife, ruling their children and their own houses well.*
>
> *For they that have used the office of a deacon well purchase to themselves a good degree, and great boldness in the faith which is in Christ Jesus.*

Deacons are elected by the church body and ordained by the pastor and fellow deacons. In most Baptist churches, only pastors and deacons are ordained. In Baptist life, deacons can function in one of two ways: as an administrative board (similar to a board of directors in a corporation) or as a ministering body (similar to the ministering organized and carried out by a Latter-day Saint elders quorum). The deacons in our church were a ministering body, responsible for helping the pastor minister to the needs of our congregation. The deacons of our congregation were also a great sounding board for me to use any time I needed input on a decision I had to make regarding the church. I was fortunate to serve with some good men in our deacon body.

The Women's Ministry leader (or WMU leader) functions in much the way a Relief Society president functions, coordinating the women's ministry in the church. They also promote the work of our missionaries around the world and help coordinate offerings to fund the missionaries' work.

The treasurer keeps a record of the tithes and offerings and pays the bills. The Sunday School director selects and purchases the Sunday School curriculum that is taught every quarter.

Once a month (later we changed to once a quarter) we had a business meeting where we received the reports of the various ministries of the church. We also voted on various items of business that needed the full congregation's approval for action. Every member of the congregation could vote on these issues.

ORDINANCES

There are two ordinances in the Southern Baptist church—baptism and The Lord's Supper (akin to Sacrament). Though these ordinances are important and significant aspects of membership in a Baptist church, they are not viewed as saving ordinances. Baptists believe the Lord has commanded us to perform these ordinances. They are symbols of the great work of our Lord Jesus Christ. But they are only symbols, they are not required for salvation. Baptists practice "believers" baptism—they only baptize those who profess faith (believe) in Jesus Christ. There is no set age for this ordinance. Whenever a congregation feels a person has made a definite commitment to Jesus Christ, they can be baptized. Baptists practice baptism by immersion. The performance of the ordinance is virtually the same as that of the Church. In most cases the baptistry is in the chapel, and the ordinance is usually performed as part of a worship service.

In most Baptist churches, the ordinance of the Lord's Supper is not observed weekly. There is no set schedule. The church I pastored observed the Lord's Supper once every three months. We sometimes had special observances on Easter and Christmas. At Mt. Zion Baptist Church, the pastor and the deacons administered the Lord's Supper. The pastor usually read the account of the Lord's Supper from scripture. He would ask a deacon to say the blessing (there were no prescribed prayers) on the bread. The bread consisted of small, individually portioned pieces of unleavened bread. The deacons took trays and distributed them to members of the congregation. Once every member had a piece of unleavened bread, we would, following the pastor's lead, eat the bread at the same time. Next, we followed the same process with the cup. A deacon blessed the tray containing small cups (like our sacrament cups) of grape juice. They were then passed out, and the congregation partook as one.[18]

AUTHORITY

"Where do you get your authority?" was a question I was frequently asked by missionaries and members of The Church of Jesus Christ of Latter-day Saints. I've thought a lot about this question over my years as a pastor and even after I became a member of the Church. Was my ministry in the Baptist church invalid because I didn't hold the priesthood? I finally had a wonderful discussion about authority with my stake president and Area Seventy. They affirmed with me that I did have a certain level of authority as a Baptist pastor. God called me into the ministry. He called me to pastor, so there had to be some sort of inherent authority to go along with that calling. If God calls you to do something, He will give you the tools you need to perform the task. To be sure, I did not hold the Melchizedek or Aaronic priesthoods as a pastor, and I never claimed to hold those priesthoods. I did not have the authority to baptize for the remission of sins or to lay hands on someone for the gift of the Holy Ghost. I did not have the authority to perform temple ordinances. Baptists do not claim to hold that authority! But if God called me to pastor, inherent in that calling is the type of authority I needed to minister in a Baptist church.

I see three different types of authority in a Baptist church. The first type of authority is from God, the basic authority inherent in a calling from God. The second type of authority is from the congregation. When the members of Mt. Zion Baptist Church called me as their pastor, they affirmed the calling of God on my life and the authority He had given me. They then gave me the "authority" to pastor them, to administer their church ordinances and to oversee their congregation. When I resigned as pastor of the Mt. Zion Baptist Church, I

18. For more information on the Southern Baptist understanding of these ordinances see the Baptist Faith & Message (2000) at https://bfm.sbc.net/bfm2000/#vii-baptism-and-the-lords-supper.

still had the authority inherent to my calling, but I no longer had the authority to oversee that congregation.

From my Baptist perspective, the third type of authority is scripture. The Old and New Testament are the primary medium through which Southern Baptist leaders receive "revelation." As a pastor preaches and acts according to the Bible, he is exercising the authority of God. 2 Timothy 3:16 declares that the scriptures are "given by inspiration of God." They are the words of God and are imbued with the authority of God. Baptists believe that the apostolic authority held by Peter, Paul, and the other Apostles is inherent in their writings which have been preserved in the Bible. Baptist Theologian, David Dockery writes,

> *In fulfillment of Christs promises (see John 14;26; 16:13) the apostles' authority has been placed permanently in their writings. Thus, the Spirit of God has inspired the prophetic-apostolic writings, and the Scriptures become the recognized authority that communicates God's truth, which is to be taught, believed, and obeyed.*[19]

Noted New Testament authority, F.F. Bruce wrote:

> *"The Gospels, recording 'all that Jesus began both to do and to teach,' could not be regarded as one whit lower in authority than the Old Testament books. And the teaching of the apostles in the Acts and Epistles was regarded as vested with His [Jesus] authority."*[20]

Baptists believe that as you act in accordance with scripture, you are acting under the authority of the ancient apostles and prophets. This then is one of the great distinctions between Restored Christianity and Protestant Christianity. Protestant Christianity teaches that apostolic authority resides only in the Bible. Restored Christianity believes that the authority and office of modern prophets and apostles have been restored to the earth.

---

19. David S. Dockery, *Christian Scripture*, (Nashville, TN: Broadman & Holman, 1995), 70.
20. FF. Bruce, *The New Testament Documents*, 5th ed. Rev., (Grand Rapids, MI: Eerdmans, 1992), 26.

PAID CLERGY

When you consider that a Baptist pastor has to function as the leader of a small corporation, in addition to preaching, teaching, and ministering, it might provide a little more insight into why Baptist churches have a paid clergy. Scriptures that used to support this idea include 1 Timothy 5:17–18, Leviticus 10:12–15, and Numbers 18:21 (see also 1 Corinthians 9:9).

When I started pastoring Mt. Zion Baptist Church, I was paid to be a full-time minister of the church. But as time went on and different economic forces began to bear upon the church, I voluntarily took a series of pay cuts so that the church could remain solvent. Eventually, I did get an additional job to supplement the pay from the church. When a pastor works a second job, he is considered a "bi-vocational" minister. Most Baptist pastors today are bi-vocational.

Bibliography

Works Cited

Bruce, F. F. *The New Testament Documents*, 5th ed. Rev. Grand Rapids, MI: Eerdmans, 1992.

Decker, Ed, and Dave Hunt. *The God Makers: A Shocking Expose of What the Mormon Church Really Believes*. Eugene, OR: Harvest House, 1984.

Dockery, David S. *Christian Scripture*. Nashville, TN: Broadman & Holman. 1995.

Hinckley, Gordon B. "The Marvelous Foundation of Our Faith." *The Church of Jesus Christ of Latter-Day Saints*, www.churchofjesuschrist.org/study/general-conference/2002/10/the-marvelous-foundation-of-our-faith?lang=eng. Accessed 23 April 2020.

__________. *Truth Restored*. Salt Lake City, UT: Corporation of the President of The Church of Jesus Christ of Latter-day Saints, 1979.

Keetch, Elder Von G. "Blessed and Happy Are Those Who Keep the Commandments of God." *The Church of Jesus Christ of Latter-Day Saints*, 2015. www.churchofjesuschrist.org/study/general-conference/2015/10/blessed-and-happy-are-those-who-keep-the-commandments-of-god?lang=eng. Accessed 23 April 2020.

Lewis, C. S. *The Screwtape Letters: and Screwtape Proposes a Toast*. New York: HarperOn, An Imprint of HarperCollins Publishers, 2013.

Patterson, W. Morgan. *William Heth Whitsitt: The Seminary's Versatile Scholar.* 1994 TMs.Special Collections, The Southern Baptist Theological Seminary. Louisville, KY.

Ready, Bryan. *William H. Whitsitt: Insights into Early Mormonism.* 2001. sidneyrigdon.com/books/2001Read.htm. Accessed 23 April 2020.

Richards, LeGrand. *A Marvelous Work and a Wonder.* Salt Lake City, UT: Deseret Book Company, 1972.

Rogers, Adrian. "Faith In Jesus...Not Faith In Faith." *Love Worth Finding Ministries*, 20 Apr. 2017, www.lwf.org/daily-devotions/faith-in-jesus-not-faith-in-faith. Accessed 18 September 2020.

Rogers, Adrian, and Steve Rogers. *What Every Christian Ought to Know.* Nashville, TN: B & H Publishing Group, 2014.

Sproul, R C. *Chosen by God.* Orlando, FL: Ligonier Ministries, 1984.

"Southern Baptist Convention." *The Baptist Faith and Message*, 2000, www.sbc.net/bfm2000/bfm2000.asp. Accessed 23 April 2020.

Schaff, Philip. "Athanasian Creed." *Wikipedia*, Wikimedia Foundation, 14 Apr. 2020, en.wikipedia.org/wiki/Athanasian Creed. Accessed 23 April 2020.

Sharp, Thomas. Editorial. Warsaw Signal. May 29, 1844.

__________. "Unparalleled Outrage at Nauvoo." Warsaw Signal. June 12, 1844.

Smith, Joseph Jr. "Letter to William W. Phelps, 22 July 1840," p. 158, The Joseph Smith Papers, accessed April 23, 2020, https://www.josephsmithpapers.org/paper-summary/letter-to-william-w-phelps-22-july-1840/2.

Talmage, James E. *A Study of the Articles of Faith: Being a Consideration of the Principal Doctrines of the Church of Jesus Christ of Latter-day Saints.* Salt Lake City, UT: Church of Jesus Christ of Latter-Day Saints, 1972.

__________. *Jesus the Christ: A Study of the Messiah and His Mission According to Holy Scriptures Both Ancient and Modern.* Salt Lake City, UT: Deseret Book Co., 1966.

The Holy Bible (King James Version). The Book of Mormon: Another Testament of Jesus Christ. The Doctrine and Covenants of The Church of Jesus Christ of Latter-Day Saints. The Pearl of Great Price. Salt Lake City, UT: The Church of Jesus Christ of Latter-day Saints, 2013.

Whitsitt, William H., *Sidney Rigdon: The Real Founder of Mormonism.* 1886. rev. 1891. TMs. (on-line). Accessed 25, September 2000. Available from http://sidneyrigdon.com/wht/1891WhtB.htm; Internet.

Recommended Reading

Books that have been very helpful to me during my investigation of The Church of Jesus Christ of Latter-day Saints and/or my relationship with Jesus Christ.

The Holy Bible (King James Version). The Book of Mormon: Another Testament of Jesus Christ. The Doctrine and Covenants of The Church of Jesus Christ of Latter-Day Saints. The Pearl of Great Price. Salt Lake City, UT: The Church of Jesus Christ of Latter-day Saints, 2013.

Blomberg, Craig, and Stephen E. Robinson. *How Wide the Divide?: a Mormon & an Evangelical in Conversion.* Downers Grove, IL: InterVarsity Press, 1997.

Brown, Joan Winmill. *Day by Day with Billy Graham.* Minneapolis, MN: World Wide Publications, 1976.

Gaskill, Alonzo L. *Converted: True Mormon Conversion Stories from 15 Religions.* Springville, UT: CFI, an Imprint of Cedar Fort, Inc., 2017.

Grudem, Wayne. *Systematic Theology: An Introduction to Biblical Doctrine.* Downers Grove, IL: InterVarsity, 2007

Lund, Gerald N. *The Work and the Glory.* 9 Volumes. Salt Lake City, UT: Bookcraft, Inc., 1990–1998.

Millet, Robert L., and Gregory C. V. Johnson. *Bridging the Divide: The Continuing Conversation between a Mormon and an Evangelical.* Rhinebeck, NY: Monkfish Book Pub. Co., 2007.

Millet, Robert L., and Shon Hopkin. *Mormonism: A Guide for the Perplexed.* London: Bloomsbury Academic, 2015.

Oaks, Dallin H., and Marvin S. Hill. *Carthage Conspiracy: The Trial of the Accused Assassins of Joseph Smith.* Urbana, IL: University of Illinois Press, 1975.

Preach My Gospel: A Guide to Missionary Service. Salt Lake City, UT: Church of Jesus Christ of Latter-Day Saints,2004.

Saints: The Story of the Church of Jesus Christ in the Latter Days. Vol 1 & 2. Salt Lake City, UT: The Church of Jesus Christ of Latter-day Saints, 2018.

Shipps, Jan. *Mormonism: The Story of a New Religious Tradition.* Urbana IL: University of Illinois Press, 1985.

Spurgeon, C. H. *Morning & Evening.* New Kensington, PA: Whitaker House, 2002.

Woodworth, Jed, and Richard L. Bushman. *Joseph Smith: Rough Stone Rolling.* New York: Alfred A. Knopf, 2005.

About the Author

Bryan E. Ready has a bachelor of arts in religion as well as a master of divinity and master of theology. Prior to joining the Church in 2016, Bryan made several trips to Nauvoo, Illinois, and fell in love with Church history. He studied Church history and theology for over thirty years. He is a member of the Mormon Historical Association. Bryan also served as a Southern Baptist minister for twenty-five years. During his time as a minister, he often spoke about the Church to other Southern Baptists and facilitated dialogues between the members of the two churches. Bryan has been married for twenty-six years and is the father of six children.